D1065138

Drucker on Asia

The idea alone is good: two old men, the American management guru Peter F. Drucker and the Japanese tycoon Isao Nakauchi, enter into a dialogue. The book that emerges from this is even better...Drucker knows so much, and views the economic situation more from the outside. Nakauchi can do so much, which means of course that he is right in the thick of it. An ideal mix for all future entrepreneurs, as the founders of tomorrow must achieve both: theoretical reflection and hands-on creativity.'

Manager, Germany

Drucker on Asia

A dialogue
between Peter Drucker and Isao Nakauchi

Peter F. Drucker • Isao Nakauchi

Butterworth-Heinemann
Linacre House, Jordan Hill, Oxford OX2 8DP
313 Washington Street, Newton, MA 02158-1626
A division of Reed Educational and Professional Publishing Ltd

-Q A member of the Reed Elsevier plc group

OXFORD BOSTON JOHANNESBURG
MELBOURNE NEW DELHI SINGAPORE

First published in Japanese in two volumes as *Chosen no toki* by
Diamond, Inc., Tokyo, 1995
First published in Great Britain 1997

British Library Cataloguing in Publication Data
A catalogue record for this book is available from the British
Library

Library of Congress Cataloguing in Publication Data
A catalogue record for this book is available from the Library of
Congress

ISBN 0 7506 3132 5

Typeset by Intercultural Networking Ltd, London
Printed in the United States of America

Contents

Part II – Time to Reinvent

Preface

Peter F. Drucker

I AM WRITING THIS PREFACE on March 11, 1995 – ten years to the day since the collapse of Communism and of the Soviet Empire began with Mikhail Gorbachev's election as the First Secretary of the Communist Party. The political world has changed beyond all recognition in these ten years. But, while less dramatic, the changes in the economic world have been fully as great, fully as important, fully as irreversible. And far too little attention is being paid to them.

Specifically, government has become the storm center of the non-communist world, threatening sudden, unpredictable economic and currency upheavals – the legacy of forty years of failure of the 'Keynesian Welfare State' whose theories and policies dominated the Western non-communist world before 1985. These threats – and especially the threat of sudden panic and collapse undoing years of hard, steady work on economic development and prosperity such as only a few months ago occurred in Mexico – are by no means confined to developing countries. Sweden and Italy, to name only two European countries, are equally unstable as a result of government over-spending and over-borrowing. Even France's stability is doubtful. And the US is engaged in a massive last-ditch attempt to cut its government deficit. While Japan – alone of all major countries in the developed world – has not indulged in the reckless expansion of government spending and in under-saving grossly, her government and policies too are in crisis. Forty years of stability have come to an end. And no country is as exposed to the shock waves which a collapse of government finance and currencies creates as is Japan – *endaka* is just a foretaste of what a collapse of the Chinese economy and Chinese currency under the threat of run-away inflation might, for instance, mean to Japan.

Secondly, the structure and the dynamics of the world economy have changed profoundly. The 'growth economies' of the world in the last ten years have not been Japan or the US or Western Europe. They have been the rapidly developing countries of mainland Asia – with Coastal China in the forefront – and some countries of Latin America which, returning to fiscal rectitude and free markets after years of wild inflation and protectionism, have shown almost explosive (though also very dangerous) growth. There is no one 'economic center' in the world economy any more; the tiny island of Taiwan has now the world's second-largest foreign-exchange surplus. And there are no 'superpowers'. Japan leads in the development of mainland Asia. But in the high-tech industries where the real growth is – biotechnology and genetics, information technology, software, the new finance – Japan is still sadly lagging. The US has put its manufacturing house in order. Most of US manufacturing industry is now as competitive as that of any other country; even the automotive industry has almost caught up. And the US has attained an almost unbeatable lead in the new growth industries, and especially in the high-tech industries. But government finance and the savings rate are in sorry shape.

Western Europe has not been able to exploit the enormous opportunities of economic unification and has fallen badly behind in manufacturing efficiency in all high-tech areas, and in employment.

Thirdly, organization structure and business strategies are in flux. Information is beginning to affect both, to the point where traditional business organization is becoming obsolete. But also the traditional concept of the 'employer' – the company for which people work – is unravelling. More and more people work as temporaries. Outsourcing is becoming general. In outsourcing people work *with* a company, for example doing its data processing, but do not work *for* the company, and are not its employees. In the West – though apparently not yet in Japan – more and more of the most senior and most responsible employees, such as senior researchers, rarely even come to the company's office any more but work at home or in small office clusters close to where they live.

Fourthly, the work force is changing rapidly. Blue-collar industrial workers in the mass-production plants were the center of the work force only yesterday. Today, they are shrinking rapidly in numbers and, even more rapidly, in importance. Even the people who do the jobs in the plant which the blue-collar worker did yesterday, are increasingly different people. They are 'technicians' with a substantial theoretical knowledge rather than people who get paid for working with their hands or for tending machines. And at the center of gravity of the work force in every developed country are increasingly knowledge workers, people who do not work with their hands at all but are being paid for what they have learned in school and university. These people have totally different expectations – of their work; of the way they are being managed; of their opportunities and rewards. But also the measures that made traditional blue-collar workers productive do not work to make knowledge workers productive. They pose a different, but no less critical, productivity challenge.

And fifthly, underlying all this is the shift to *knowledge* as the key resource of production.

What happened in the last ten years is not that free markets and free enterprise won. Communism and central planning collapsed. But this only brought out all the more clearly the challenges which free markets and free enterprise now face.

What then does all this mean for an individual country and its economy – and specifically for Japan? For society? For the individual company? And, finally, for the individual, and especially for the individual executive or professional? These are the questions to which the dialogue between Mr Nakauchi and myself addressed itself. The dialogue started last Autumn on my most recent visit to Japan. It was then continued during the Autumn and Winter by letter and fax. Mr Nakauchi and I share the same concerns, but we tackle them differently: Mr Nakauchi as a Japanese, though one with intimate knowledge of the West; as an entrepreneur who has built and runs the Daiei Company, one of the world's largest and most successful food retailers; and as a businessman deeply concerned through his leadership in *Keidanren* (where he is Vice Chairman) with public policy and with society. I approach the same concerns as a Westerner – though as one who knows a little bit about Japan and deeply loves the country. I am not a 'theoretician'; through my consulting practice I am in daily touch with the concrete opportunities and problems of a fairly large number of institutions, foremost among them businesses but also hospitals, government agencies and public-service institutions such as museums and universities. And I am working with such institutions on several continents: North America, including Canada and Mexico; Latin America; Europe; Japan and South East Asia. Still, a consultant is at one remove from the day-to-day practice – that is both his strength and his weakness. And so my viewpoint tends more to be that of an outsider. The two approaches, however, complement each other as Mr Nakauchi and I soon found out.

This dialogue is presented in two parts because that is how it was conducted. The first part looks at the major developments in economy, society and business. The second then focuses on the specific challenge of a period of transition such as ours: *how to change and renew – oneself as an individual? one's business? government?* But both parts have in common a conviction that Mr Nakauchi and I share: theory and practice have to go together. Theory tells us *what* needs to be done. Practice then tells us *how* to do it. Throughout this dialogue Mr Nakauchi and I have tried to provide both understanding and effective action. There are many questions a reader will ask which neither of us could answer – we are still in mid-transition. But I hope that there is enough in this dialogue to enable each reader both to obtain much deeper understanding of our rapidly changing world and effective guidance to his own action, learning, improvement, and growth, and to better performance of his business.

The initiative for this dialogue came from Mr Nakauchi, and so did the formulation of the main questions. I am deeply grateful to him for the searching thinking that went into his questions and for the foundation for a productive dialogue which his extensive comments laid. But thanks are due to some other people too, who, during the course of the project, constantly advised and challenged us: to Mr Tatsuo Fukuda, Mr Shinichi Uesaka and Mr Katsuyoshi Saito, respectively Publisher, Editor and Foreign Rights General Manager at Diamond Publishing, Inc. in Tokyo. The project owes to these three gentlemen a great deal of its cohesion and clarity. They deserve our and the reader's thanks.

Peter F. Drucker
Claremont, California

Part I

Times of Challenge

1

The challenges of China

What is the future for China's huge market?
Isao Nakauchi

RECENT ECONOMIC DEVELOPMENTS in Asia are fascinating, especially those in China. That country's rapid growth and transformation amaze us all. China exerts a kind of magnetic attraction for investment by companies from around the world, in direct contrast to Russia, for example. The source of this magnetism is China's huge market of somewhere between 1.2 and 1.5 billion inhabitants. While Russia started its entry to the modern world by changing its political system, the Chinese government has succeeded in transforming its economy first, by adopting open policies that are extremely flexible and realistic. It must be said, of course, that China's market socialism, and its approach to human rights, are not easily understandable for us outsiders. The world's entrepreneurs find that evaluation of the potential of the Chinese market is a matter of considerable strategic importance.

Professor Drucker, I would like to seek your views on the China of today and tomorrow.

September 21, 1994

3

China offers greater dangers than any other market ... and opportunities too great to be ignored
Peter Drucker

WHAT YOU, AT DAIEI – and a few other mass retailers in Japan – have done in the last few decades is a great deal more than to build major new businesses. You have, through your business enterprise, tackled and solved what only forty years ago was one of Japan's central social problems, seemingly an intractable one – how to convert yesterday's Mom-and-Pop stores into a modern distribution system, without major social dislocation. I mention this right at the outset because so many of the questions in our dialogue deal with social dislocations caused by changes in world economy, world society and world politics, fully as much as by technology. The way in which you at Daiei, and a few other retailers in Japan, have used these dislocations as opportunities, both to build major businesses and to solve social problems, is the example we need to tackle the dislocation problems which threaten to become so important and so difficult in the years to come.

Growing Coastal China

And now, let me turn to the questions which you have raised in your letter.

I think it is appropriate that your first question deals with China and its future. For surely the emergence of Coastal China and of mainland South-east Asia during the last ten or fifteen years is the most important event in the world economy. But it also raises the most questions.

All of us know that within the last decade or so, Coastal China has been the fastest growing area in the world economy growing as fast as any area has ever grown before. Statistics about China are notoriously unreliable, but there is every reason to believe that Coastal China has already become the world's number three economic power. If it continues on its present course, it will have become the world's number two economic power by the year 2000, producing as much as Japan does now or more, though with three or four times the population. In fact, the emergence of Coastal China as an economic power has totally changed the very nature of the world economy.

From 'triad' to multi-centric world economy

Only a few short years ago, one of the ablest students of the world economy, your countryman, Kenichi Ohmae, told us that the only part of the world that matters is what he called the "triad" – the developed countries of Japan, North America and Western Europe. We need not, he assured us, pay much attention to the developing world. The decisions will be made in the countries of the triad. The countries of the triad will also be the only markets that really matter.

At the time – about ten years ago or so – this seemed an eminently realistic perspective and, in fact, a needed antidote to the romantic view of 'development' that had prevailed in the 1960s and 1970s. But it has turned out to be wrong. There is no more centre in the world economy; it has become multi-centric. The main event bringing this about was, of course, the explosive growth of Coastal China and the rapid development of other South-east Asian countries – Korea, Thailand, Malaysia, Indonesia, the Philippines. Away from Asia, similar development has occurred in Latin America, beginning with the 'Mexican Miracle,' that is with the turn around in Mexico that started immediately upon the stabilisation of the currency and the freeing of the capital markets. Similar explosive growth started in whatever country in Latin American followed Mexico's example: stopping inflation and opening up capital markets. First Chile, then Argentina, then Peru, have had growth rates quite similar to those of South-east Asia. It would take very little in Brazil to bring about similar explosive growth.

Developed countries suffering with 'flu

This is all the more remarkable because, during the last decade, the developed countries, the countries of the triad, have not done so well. Japan, as I will be discussing a little later, has indeed done very much better than most of you in Japan believe. There is very little reason, in my opinion, for the pessimism which I found so widespread in Japan during my last visit there this past autumn. The United States has also actually done a great deal better than most people believe, either in Japan or in the US. These have nevertheless been difficult and turbulent times, both in Japan and in the US. Western Europe has actually been in a severe recession and has lost growth momentum. Yet world trade has grown as fast as ever before, if not faster. So has world production.

Anyone, ten years ago, would have considered this impossible. It has been an axiom of economics – I would say for almost four hundred years – that if the developed countries have as much as the slightest head cold, the developing world collapses. The developed world these last ten years has had a pretty bad head cold – I would call it a fairly nasty 'flu. Yet, in many parts of the world and especially in Mainland Asia, these have been unprecedented boom times. This is something which no economic theory can yet explain, but it is a fact. As a result, the world economy has ceased to be dominated by the economic powers of the triad, which Kenichi Ohmae, only ten years ago, considered to be in total control.

Shifts in the balance of economic power

Taiwan, a small island without natural resources, has today the second largest capital hoard in the world. China is already becoming a major automobile market, with Germany's Volkswagen and Japan's Toyota fighting hard for its leadership. The world's largest producer of room air-conditioners, a highly engineered product, is now in Singapore. And the world's largest producers of standard micro-circuit 'chips' are in Korea and Taiwan.

It should be underlined that developments in South America have shifted the balance of power. When the North American Free Trade Agreement (NAFTA) was signed in 1992, a great many people, both in Mexico and in the United States, predicted that Mexican business and industry would be taken over, swallowed up by American 'multi-nationals.' Actually, it is the Mexicans who have been moving into the United States. There has been more investment by Mexican companies in the southern and western United States in the last two to three years than there has been US investment in Mexico. Businesses which, by their nature, require small plants because their products cannot be shipped very far – such as cement or glass bottles – are now almost completely owned by Mexican companies in the southern and south-western United States.

A multi-centric world

Another equally amazing fact: Germany's recovery, after six years of stagnation and severe recession, did not begin with a revival of the domestic market. It did not begin with exports to Germany's traditional best customers, its neighbours in the European Union. It did not begin with exports to the traditional customers for Germany's best products, its high-value-added, high-priced engineering products. It began with exports to mainland Asia, and especially exports to Mainland China.

In other words, the world has become multi-centric with a vengeance. This is the first thing to say about the importance of China. Because, in this total restructuring of the world economy, the central event is clearly the emergence of Coastal China as a major economic power.

Secrets of Chinese management

Unless there is a collapse of China, I would predict that within ten years or so we will see as many books in the United States and Europe entitled 'Secrets of Chinese Management' as, during the last ten years, we have seen books entitled 'Secrets of Japanese Management.' The Chinese are developing a distinct and quite different management style and management structure. I have often said that the secret of Japan consists in Japan's ability to make a family out of the modern corporation. The secret of Chinese management may well consist in the ability of the Chinese to make the family into a modern corporation.

Overseas Chinese

I would argue that in the last few years a new economic super-power has arisen, and one for which we have no precedent at all: the Overseas Chinese. They are scattered in a great many locations, and along both sides of the Pacific. There are Hong Kong, Taiwan and Singapore – three small places with populations entirely or at least predominantly Chinese. There is equally Malaysia, in which people of Chinese stock constitute 30 per cent of the population; and the Philippines, Indonesia, and Thailand, in which people of Chinese extraction are an even smaller percentage; and there are, of course, Overseas Chinese on my side of the Pacific, in Vancouver, Canada; in San Francisco, and in a good many places in California. These Chinese are loyal citizens of whatever country they live in, yet they also constitute an invisible economic network that is held together by ties of kinship and family. It is held together by the mutual trust of family members which, through China's long history, was the only way in which a family could survive and preserve some money. Again, this is a new, major development, and one that deserves to be studied and taken very seriously. The Overseas

Chinese are rapidly building new multi-nationals, based primarily on family connections, and often without any major investment of money.

An example of a company run by people of Chinese extraction

One example is a Bangkok-based company which manufactures parts for major makers of personal computers all over the world. It is owned and run by a Thai citizen of Chinese ancestry. It now has eleven plants world-wide: three in mainland China, four in the United States, three in Malaysia, and one in Indonesia, and is planning to build two or three additional plants in Europe in 1995, probably in the UK. Every one of these plants is run by a citizen of the country in which it operates. But every one of these plant managers is of Chinese extraction and is related by blood to the owner or to the owner's wife. The only exception is the head of US operations, who is an American of German extraction, but who is married to the niece of the Bangkok owner. None of these eleven plants is big, nor will the ones in Europe be big. Each employs no more than a hundred or a hundred and fifty people. But together, the particular parts they make now supply practically every major computer manufacturer in the world, with a market share that approaches 50 per cent.

Investment in 'invisible infrastructure'

The great importance of the Overseas Chinese is their contribution to mainland China. Manufacturers from the developed countries, with the Japanese in the lead, are the main investors in heavy capital equipment – manufacturing plants, and the rebuilding of railroads, telecommunications, and so on. The Overseas Chinese, however, focus on the 'invisible infrastructure.' They are building a financial network. China has practically no financial infrastructure, and needs it badly. They supply a good deal of distribution, especially in the interior of China, and especially outside the major metropolitan areas. They are also supplying whatever legal basis there will be – and without a legal basis, China will simply be incapable of developing.

A shortage of educated people

Even more important, the Overseas Chinese are the only ones able to supply China's greatest and most crucial need: educated people.

Everyone who has done business in China has found Chinese workers highly receptive to training, but the real strength of a modern economy is not a workforce. We know how to train workers, and in a short time. The real strength is a critical mass of educated people: engineers, accountants, market researchers, chemists, metallurgists, financial analysts, and so on. These are practically unknown in China. China is way behind in both the quantity and the quality of people with advanced education. Altogether, China, a country of 1.2 billion people has only 4 million students in institutions of higher learning beyond secondary school. The US, with not much more than one-fifth the population of China, has 12.5 million. Japan, with not much more than one-tenth the population of China, has at least 5 million people in tertiary education. In China, the educated people – never very many, let alone enough – were almost wiped out by the Cultural Revolution.

Higher education in China

What is equally serious is that most of the young people in Chinese universities today are being educated to be useless. They are being educated to be government economists and bureaucrats. They are being educated to be yesterday's mandarins, whose greatest pride was that they knew nothing useful and never dirtied their hands with anything that could possibly be construed as productive work. To create an educated labour force is not simply a matter of training, and cannot be done in a few months or even a few years. In Japan the effort began in the early years of Meiji; it was not until the end of Meiji before the country had a supply of educated people adequate to its needs, and that was only eighty years ago.

This is where the Overseas Chinese are making their greatest contribution. Capital and technology can be supplied from abroad. Perhaps even top management can be supplied from abroad, although only for a short period. But middle management, professionals, technologists, have to be natives of the country in which they operate, or at least part of the same culture. In China they cannot be supplied from Japan or from the US or from Europe. They have to be supplied by people who see themselves as Chinese and are accepted as Chinese. And this is where the Overseas Chinese will become the critical, in fact the decisive, element in the development of the Chinese economy and society.

Confucians in the modern world

We can project, I think, what China will look like if it continues its economic growth for another five, ten or fifteen years – the most optimistic assumption. If we can be optimistic about China, the China of 2010 is likely to be a very traditional China and yet, a very modern China. It may well be governed, as China has been throughout its history, by a small cadre of mandarins. Indeed, in my trips to China, I have always felt that the so-called communist 'elite,' that is, the people in the governing party and in the government itself, are no different from the Confucians who governed China for most of its history. Like their ancestors, they are totally devoid of any practical experience. In fact, they are contemptuous of practical experience. They believe in pure theory, considering it beneath their dignity to concern themselves with worldly matters such as running a business. It is no accident that there is practically no state-owned industry in China which is run properly, which is well-managed, and which can produce a decent product that people actually want to buy. All the development in the last ten or fifteen years has come from the private sector, as you know, and practically all of it has come from enterprises that manage to divorce themselves from management, or even from supervision, by the eroding bureaucracy.

Underneath this impotent and incompetent Confucian class – and in a way it is no different from the mandarins of Imperial China over thousands of years – there would then be a thriving economy run largely by the family networks into which the Overseas Chinese are rapidly organising themselves. At the bottom, as always in China, would then be a peasantry – in fifteen years from now, perhaps a productive one, although I admit this is perhaps more optimism than the facts can sustain.

Optimism ... China's potential as an organisation of autonomous regions

While still legally one country with a central government, the actual reality – as so often during Chinese history – would be a country that is organised more or less openly, in what historically used to be territories of warlords, and are now called 'Autonomous Economic Regions'. These are large regional groupings, populated by people who all speak more or less the same dialect, whether that of Shanghai, or of Canton, or of Amoy, and are governed from one dominant, regional city. They pay lip service to the central government but very little else, being more or less in control of their own affairs. Each of these regions would be as large as any but the largest countries in the world. And each would have a very distinct character. This, historically, has been the pattern of Chinese organisation, and, in fact, China has flourished the most when this pattern has prevailed.

There are strong signs that this is the pattern towards which China is already moving. There are already five of these 'Autonomous Economic Regions' in existence, though not yet officially. One of these is emerging in Manchuria. Another one around Tientsin. One around Shanghai. One around the Canton-Hong Kong axis. And finally, one around Taiwan-Amoy.

This, I submit, is a most optimistic projection for China for the year 2010. Or, rather, what is optimistic is to expect that this development will happen peacefully, harmoniously, and without major upheaval or catastrophe. Is it too optimistic?

'Bubble economy' in China

It is predictable, in fact practically certain, that China will undergo severe turbulence within the next few years. No country that has ever developed as fast as has Mainland China can possibly escape a severe shake-up. Bubbles, as Japan has learned painfully, always burst. In a few years we will certainly talk of the bursting of China's bubble economy – and the bubble is both much bigger and more extended than the bubble that burst in Japan a few years ago. Will this just be a temporary turbulence or will China enter a period of prolonged and serious crisis, perhaps even a period of prolonged and serious civil war?

The issue of Deng Xiaoping's succession

The great question is not the one that is most often discussed in our newspapers: the succession to the old men who came in with the Communist Revolution almost fifty years ago, and who are going to leave the stage of history within the next few years. To be sure, the basic problem in any autocracy is that there is no organised process for succession. It is decided by brute force. But perhaps it does not greatly matter who is at the top in China. Real control may already have slipped out of the hands of the central government, and out of Beijing altogether.

Inflation and social upheaval

Far more serious, are two other questions. First, there is the terrible choice China faces between inflation and severe social upheaval. Inflation, now running at about 30 percent a year, has twice before destroyed Chinese dynasties. The first time was 350 years ago when inflation destroyed the Ming Dynasty. That inflation began in Europe around 1500, when silver from America began to flood all European countries. Within a hundred years it destroyed the flourishing economy of the late Renaissance, with its multi-national merchant cities such as those of the Hanseatic League in Northern Europe, Florence, Genoa, and Barcelona in Southern Europe. It then ushered in the age of the absolute monarchy. Finally, around 1600, the inflation spread to China. It depreciated the silver on which the Chinese economy was based. The Ming Dynasty paid its soldiers in silver, but the Manchu had access to the gold in the rivers of Northern Manchuria and, thus, they could bribe the Ming Dynasty soldiers to make them defect. This, within a short twenty-five years, led to the collapse of the Ming Dynasty and its overthrow by the Manchu.

Three hundred years later, in the years during and following the Pacific War, inflation led to the overthrow of the new 'dynasty,' the Kuomintang, headed by Chiang Kai-shek. For Chiang Kai-shek was not defeated by Mao's armies. He was defeated by inflation which made his soldiers desert by the thousands and, in the end, by the millions. No one in Beijing has forgotten that.

Unemployment in state-owned enterprises

The alternative to inflation may be even worse. For inflation in China today is being caused by the total incompetence and unproductivity of the state-owned enterprises. Practically every one of them is bankrupt and practically none of them produces goods anybody wants to buy. And yet, they employ 100,000,000 people, or half of all people at work outside farming. Without the government's printing the money that causes inflation, the state industries would have to close almost immediately. Halting inflation would mean throwing a hundred million people out of work. Can any government, let alone a communist government – supposedly a government of and by the workers – survive unemployment figures of 50 or 60 per cent in the cities?

The dilemma of Chinese government

It is on the horns of this dilemma that any Chinese government is being caught. What makes this dilemma particularly threatening is that it endangers the support of the military which, basically, is the only support the Communist government of Beijing still enjoys. Inflation threatens the army because it rapidly depreciates what soldiers and junior officers get by way of pay, and they have been, so far, the most privileged class in Communist China. Large-scale unemployment of industrial workers would equally endanger the loyalty of the army. Thus, the first question about China is whether China can somehow finesse the choice between inflation that undermines and threatens to destroy the regime, and industrial unemployment which equally threatens and undermines the regime.

Peasants without work

An even more dangerous long-term threat is that of the growing mass of unemployed peasants drifting off the farm, and having nowhere to go. Again, in Chinese history, this has led to the collapse of one dynasty after the other, beginning with the Han 2,000 years ago. Whenever large numbers of peasants were pushed off the land because there was no work for them, there was a peasant revolt in short order. Yiian was overthrown by such a peasant revolt, which brought the Ming Dynasty to power six-hundred years ago. In the nineteenth and early twentieth century, two such peasant revolts – the Taiping revolt in mid-century, and the Boxer rebellion in the early years of this century – came close to overthrowing the Manchu Dynasty. They did, in fact, lead to its demise, both by making China become a virtual colony of foreign powers – European powers as well as Japan – and by totally undermining support in China for the dynasty in all classes of the population.

There already are well over a hundred million people in China who have drifted off the farms because there was no work for them there, but who are not able to find work in the cities. There are probably another 200,000,000 people still on the farm for whom there is not work. There are about 800,000,000 people living on the farm in China, about

350,000,000 of them working. Chinese agriculture probably does not need more than 150-200,000,000 workers. Thus 150,000,000 workers and their families are basically already unemployed, even though they are still living on the land.

There is thus heightened tension between the booming economies of the cities of Coastal China, where a minority lives, and where the economy is growing at up to 20 per cent a year – with large numbers of people getting rich and even larger numbers of people getting affluent – and the growing deprivation of a countryside which no longer shows any productivity increases, and which suffers from gross overpopulation.

Great chance and great risk

Mainland China, and this means particularly the coastal areas, is thus both the most promising and the most dangerous part of the present world economy. If it succeeds in surviving the tremendous problems it faces – the choice between inflation and large-scale unemployment; the tension between an impoverished rural proletariat and growing affluence in the coastal cities – it offers greater growth prospects than any country has ever offered except the United States in the closing years of the nineteenth century, and Japan in the years following the Pacific War. But at the same time, it offers greater dangers than we have ever seen anywhere. So far, there is no sign of any effective policy to tackle the problems.

A risk one cannot afford not to take

What, then, are the implications for the businessman and, especially, the Japanese businessman? Can he disregard the opportunities of China? The answer is 'No.' Can he disregard the threats of China? The answer is again 'No.' Perhaps, for a major Japanese corporation and for a major Western business as well, to go into China is a risk one cannot afford not to take. It is a gamble, and I submit a gamble in which a negative outcome is at least as likely as a positive one. In fact, an experienced gambler would probably conclude that the odds on China's success are no better than one in three. And serious turbulence can surely be expected with odds of two in three, if not worse.

The greatest market opportunities

Yet a major business in the developed world, and especially a major manufacturing business, can probably not afford *not* to go into China, either as a direct investor or with a joint-venture partner. The opportunities: the need to develop the infrastructure rapidly; the need to develop communications rapidly, especially telecommunications; the market opportunities – even if limited to the emerging middle class of three or four hundred million people – are simply too great. At the same time, anyone going into China needs to realise that it is a gamble, and a gamble not on economics, but on politics – and to avoid gambling on politics has always been the better part of wisdom for a business.

The short-term future of China and the critical decisions will be made within the next five or ten years – probably the most important issue for the world economy and world politics. A prosperous China that at the same time has a modicum of social peace, would be the greatest market opportunity since the tremendous recovery of defeated Europe and defeated Japan in the years following the Pacific War. A China in collapse, a China perhaps even in civil war, may be the greatest danger we face.

Dangers of nuclear war

There is only one other question of such magnitude facing us today – the future of the Asiatic countries of the former Soviet empire. There the economic opportunities are so much less. There is nothing that can be compared to the Overseas Chinese as a dynamo of development. The political dangers are very great: civil war can not be ruled out in the former Soviet empire, and civil war between counties that have nuclear weapons. Yet these dangers are still less likely to upset world politics, world economy and world society than a collapse of Mainland China, with its impact on all the countries of East Asia and South-east Asia, including Japan.

November 10, 1994

Only the development of invisible infrastructures will bring prosperity to China ... and that development is our task
Isao Nakauchi

YOUR RESPONSE TO MY QUESTION was clear, logical and vigorously argued. It provided an explanation for feelings that I was unable to put into words myself. Your words seemed at first so perfect that I must confess that I was left at a loss. You see, I tried to invite you into a lively argument but your points were so strong as to leave no room for rebuttal. Your letter was the best one I ever received and left me with such complicated feelings! I hope to find stimulation in these feelings, finding ways to set out my thoughts frankly in this letter to you.

Encouragement of the answer 'No'

So now I would like to speak openly about China. As you mentioned in your letter, entrepreneurs in industrialized countries have less than one-in-three chances of succeeding there, and yet they must realize that doing business in China is one risk that must be taken. I have no doubt about this.

The Japanese mass media have recently been reporting on how companies based in Japan and other industrialized countries are, one after another, forming joint ventures or signing investment agreements in China. The media tell us that China offers great business opportunities for such companies.

However, the media are also giving us contrary messages. They make us feel that opportunities can be taken for granted, but that the risks of investing in China are very high. They also let us know every day that central and regional governments in China are changing and revoking procedures and regulations, and generally causing confusion among foreign companies. We all know that the mass media exaggerate matters with which they are obsessed. Nevertheless, the fact remains that while China offers many important business opportunities, it also provides many worrisome risks. As you suggested, expansion into China is a political gamble that many enterprises based in industrialized countries have avoided so far. One must remember that the chances of failure are higher than those of success. And as you suggested, inflation and the population problems are inherent.

It is therefore perfectly normal for some entrepreneurs to hesitate, waiting until they clearly understand the direction China will take before starting operations there. Such a wait-and-see attitude is also common among Japanese business leaders. But when we consider the situation in China, no-one can criticize these people as cowards or for losing their entrepreneurial spirit.

Yet your simple answer, 'No', to the question on whether we can ignore opportunities in China, gave me positive encouragement, as I have been thinking about expanding business into China.

Attractions of the Chinese market

China has many attractions to offer. Japanese enterprises have recognized these attractions, but it seems that they have only been attracted by the country as a manufacturing base, or as a target for exports. But what should be emphasized is the attraction China offers as a market in its own right.

One reason for this comment is that the International Monetary Fund (IMF) reckons the annual per-capita income in China in 1991 to have been US\$ 1,450. This figure is about four times the officially-announced figure from the Chinese authorities. When we consider China's population, said to be at least 1.1 billion, China turns out to be a huge market worth almost US\$ 1.6 trillion each year. It is said that China's GDP in 1990 represented, in dollar terms, two percent of the global economy. But if the calculations of the IMF are correct, the GDP of China accounts for at least six percent of the globe, ranking it third in the world behind only the US and Japan.

It is true that there is political intent behind IMF calculations to inflate the size of the economies of developing nations. Furthermore, I realize that the government of China refuses to accept IMF estimates. But what matters is not the figure itself. Although China's economy is not on a par with the economies of advanced countries, in macroeconomic terms it is gradually becoming more affluent. And the time is approaching when mass consumption will take off in Chinese society.

It is obvious to visitors to China, particularly in the coastal area. One such place is Guangdong, where close ties with Hong Kong capital have led to rapid development. Like Shang-

hai, Guangdong is transforming itself from a simple production base into a large consumption base with the full attractions of an expanding commodity market.

The future that is already here

I believe that the pull exerted by this consumer market, will
spread inland along China's two great rivers. Economic
changes along the coast have resulted in the Chinese people
hearing, seeing and understanding what economic development is and the advantages that it brings. As you suggested
in your *Managing for Results*, this is a future that is already
here. This is why I believe the pull China exerts as a market
will not diminish in the foreseeable future.

It is of course a very one-sided view and exceedingly risky
to praise events in China after looking at the rapid development occurring in a small part of such a huge country. Such
a view is even more one-sided and risky given the fact, as
you mentioned, that tension may rise between the coastal
cities which enjoy the benefits of prosperity and the interior
regions that are struggling under massive unemployment,
both visible and invisible.

Economic development has brought a measure of affluence
to only about ten percent of China. An intuition I draw from
my business experience is this: for economic development to
bring prosperity to the rest of the population – more than a
billion people – a considerable time will be required, not in
the range of five or ten years but measurable in decades. This
is probably what the Chinese government means when it
says that China is still a developing country.

Expansion of the production base is not enough

We should not condone the behaviour in China of some enterprises based in industrialized countries. They ignore the
problems in China, particularly those related to the liveli-
hood of the people, and expand their operations with only
one purpose in mind – to grab a profit from the short term
advantages of low labor costs and cheap land. We cannot
deny, of course, that costs have risen in Japan, and that production in this country has reached its limits. It is difficult,
therefore, to criticize Japanese industries, particularly manufacturers, for their expansion into China in search of a lower
cost-base. And though their aim is only to earn profit over
the short term, they do create employment opportunities

within China, so that incomes of people there rise.

The advantages of low labor costs and cheap land exist not only in China but in developing countries in general. History shows us that local economic development brings with it a gradual loss of these cost advantages. In fact, enterprises based in industrialized countries, in their search for greater advantages, are planning to expand into countries that are less developed than China, such as India, Vietnam, Laos, Cambodia and Myanmar. We know that many enterprises have already begun expanding into these countries. Meanwhile, interestingly, as you mentioned in your letter, some American companies that once took their production to low-wage countries are now shifting it back to the US.

This is why no-one can state with any certainty that China's economic development will be sustained if it must depend on the production for export of secondary manufactures. As a worst-case scenario, before the benefits of economic development have a chance to spread throughout the country, friction between regions could come to the surface and get out of control, leading to massive disturbances throughout China. For the last 20 years I have been a friend of China, and have a fear that such a calamity might occur.

You wrote that the collapse of China or the outbreak of civil war would be an unprecedented danger to China itself. It would most certainly exert a tremendously negative influence on East Asia, including Japan. On this point my own feelings are in total agreement with yours – this worst-case scenario is appalling to imagine, and must be avoided at all costs.

Improvement of the 'invisible infrastructure'

To help prevent such a horrible possibility from ever becoming reality, what can we Japanese entrepreneurs do? You provide an answer to this question by clear allusion in your letter.

It lies in the simultaneous improvements to both the 'visible' and the 'invisible' infrastructures in China. As your letter sets out, businesses based in industrialized countries have already made huge capital investments in factories, railways, telecommunications networks and so on, doing much to build up the visible or tangible infrastructure. For their part, the overseas Chinese are helping to develop the 'invisible' infrastructure formed by such elements as financial networks and

19

distribution systems.

As part of these activities, I believe that the role of Japanese entrepreneurs in China is to lend support to the efforts being made by the overseas Chinese. We should co-operate in the evolution of the invisible infrastructure. I am thinking here especially of people like me who are involved in the retail trade.

For many years I have felt that a country's distribution network should be built with the capital of the people of that country. People native to the country are more aware than anyone else of the goods produced in different parts of the country, and of distribution routes that are most efficient. This is why I used to think that local people could most easily perceive distribution problems that arise in their own country. I also used to feel that Japanese people – who are novices who cannot establish a suitable distribution network themselves at home – should refrain from meddling in the distribution affairs of other nations.

The decision to expand into China

However, many years of experience in importing goods from China have brought me many connections there. To return favors received in these year, my desire has become stronger to help modernize China's distribution system, thereby contributing, if only a little, to the creation of affluence. A project was initiated several years ago to invite five Chinese students each year to study in Japan on a scholarship program at the University of Marketing and Distribution Sciences, of which I am the Chairman. My wish is to give young Chinese people opportunities to obtain knowledge about distribution, so that after they return to China they could contribute to the modernization of distribution systems there.

Economic growth in China has, however, accelerated very rapidly in recent years. Sponsoring Chinese students in Japan is no longer enough to make an impact on the modernization of China's distribution system, to keep up with the pace of development of its secondary industries. As I have remarked before, if the underdeveloped nature of the country's distribution system causes a further gap in living standards among regions, we have no guarantee that what we fear most will not occur.

I believe that for China to avoid such a worst-case scenario a certain level of material affluence must be enjoyed, not only in one part of the country but by all citizens. This goal cannot be accomplished without modernization of the distribution system. Expressed more concretely, we must find ways to avoid concentrating commodities in certain areas. Systems must be established throughout the vastness of China so that all people can buy the goods they want, when they want, in the volumes they want, at prices they can afford. This is the same target as the 'distribution revolution' that I have been striving for in Japan.

Then the question arise: how to create a modern distribution structure? It would appear that steady, albeit extremely slow, progress is already being made in the development of the visible hardware infrastructure of railways, roads, harbors and distribution facilities. In contrast, invisible software infrastructure that must be built on this hardware – logistics construction techniques, retail stores design, effective display of products – is severely underdeveloped.

It has been decided that Daiei will soon begin to establish retail outlets in China, including some in remote inland areas. We plan to learn how to do this alongside our Chinese counterparts during the process of setting up stores across country. In this way, we hope we can help modernize Chinese distribution systems, using our extensive experience of distribution in Japan.

The mission of an entrepreneur

It was flattering to hear you praise the significance of Daiei's efforts and those of other leading Japanese distributors in addressing social imbalances in Japanese distribution systems, and your observation that these techniques could equally be applied to social imbalances in other areas of society. I was extremely pleased to receive such comments from a figure for whom I have great respect, for they reinforce my belief about the importance in expanding into China.

We will probably proceed very cautiously in China. The potential for major disruptions prior to the completion of a national network of outlets still exists. As a neighboring country, however, we cannot just sit back and watch. My own experience has led me to believe that modernization of distribution enhances quality of life for people and produces peaceful societies free from the ravages of war.

You once referred to distribution as a 'Dark Continent'. Chinese distribution systems represent not just a Dark Continent but a potential quagmire. Yet I feel that it is my duty as an entrepreneur to help modernize distribution in China, for the sake of peace in China, in Asia, and in the world.

Your reply on China has heightened my perception of the considerable responsibilities conferred on the Japanese business executives involved.

December 7, 1994

Only distribution-led economic development can create the human resources which China needs more than anything else
Peter Drucker

People, not money, develop an economy

In discussing China, you rightly point out the importance of distribution: it is rarely understood by economists, and even less by politicians. Yet distribution, rather than production, is likely to be the main engine of economic development. Development economists talk of investment-led development. They talk of export-led development. And they talk of 'distribution-led development,' that is, of development in which the economic dynamics are created in the domestic market. There are examples of all three in economic history. What distinguishes distribution-led development is that, unlike the other two, it not only develops businesses, it develops people.

The investment-led theory of development, on which the World Bank was founded fifty years ago, has not proven out in the last half-century. I say that, even though I was among the early, enthusiastic backers of the World Bank and, in fact, worked closely with its first two presidents. It has not worked because the investments of the World Bank did not produce the human resources. People, rather than money, develop an economy. World Bank investments were mostly made in big manufacturing facilities such as steel mills. While they then produced steel and jobs, such mills do not produce human competence. Distribution-led development, on the other hand, precisely because it creates hundreds and thousands of small businesses, creates human resources and human competence.

Distribution in China

In China, this may be particularly important. What China needs more than anything else are people with a little experience in starting, building, and running a business – with a little experience in managing other people, with a little experience in managing finance, and so on. They need exactly the kind of people whom your franchisees represent: local, small businessmen, who have enough support from a central organization so that their businesses are efficient and effective, and who yet have to be responsible within their own small sphere. Governments, as a rule, do not understand this. In fact, governments the world over are suspicious of the small local business precisely because it is hard to control. And Communist governments as in China are particularly unlikely to understand the dynamics of development. All bureaucrats believe in big, centralized organizations. Communism – whether in its political dimension, its social dimension, or its economic dimension – is a gospel of total centralization and of decision-making at the very top, with a minimum of local initiative or local responsibility. The last fifty years in China, therefore, have seriously undermined the country's ability to form the human capital that it needs for development. And only a distribution system can rapidly provide these resources.

In a country as vast as China distribution may well take very different forms in different areas. It may be possible that we will, in a developed China, see a dozen distribution systems, each centered around a major metropolitan area, but each autonomous, if not independent. All of them will have in common a requirement for people at the local level, that is at the level of the individual store, who are learning to run a business; who are learning to make decisions; who are learning to manage people; who, in other words, are being trained in and through their work to be the agents of economic development. What I am saying is simply that distribution is not just one element of development of China. To be sure, other things are also needed.

First, above all, a reliable and predictable legal system, and a fairly effective financial system. It was the latter, if I may say so, that provided the main energy for Japan's rapid development in the Meiji period. I consider Eiichi Shibusawa to be the central figure in Japan's economic development in the last century. But the one absolutely indispensable and central factor in the development of China will have to be a modern distribution system which develops human energies. Without them the rest is unlikely to work. For this reason, your approach to the development of China strikes me as being most thoughtful and most valid.

December 20, 1994

2

The challenges of a borderless world

What do you think about the 'hollowing out' of Japanese industry and Japan's role in a borderless world? What is the ideal arrangement of global economic blocs?
Isao Nakauchi

Japan's role in Asia

It is said that Asian countries, which have become a kind of economic growth center for the world, should involve China in efforts to create an economic bloc along the lines of NAFTA or the EU. The United States, showing some degree of concern about these developments, is participating in APEC. What one should realize, however, is that the continent of Asia shows diversity, both culturally and historically. Obviously Asian countries will continue to emphasize their individual unique characteristics. I believe that the energies emanating from Asian countries will spread out in different directions, rather than converge into one.

Meanwhile, there are people who say that Japan should assume leadership in Asia by directing its energy toward achieving such convergence. But I believe that Japan should not take a leadership role at least in the political arena. I also believe that Japan's role in Asia must have an economic motive. Japan should attempt to foster development based on the strength of each nation. This can be done by promoting a

25

horizontal division of economic specialization, and by Japan opening its markets to Asian products. Japan, of course, must not repeat the mistakes it made half a century ago, as it then professed to be the leader in Asia.

The 'hollowing out' of Japanese industry and the borderless world

In Japan some argue that economic specialization on an international scale weakens the core of Japanese industry. Yet we all know that manufacturing is most efficient when done in that part of the world where resources, technology and costs are most favorable. When products are made in optimum locations and enjoy a free-trade environment, the world's regions develop relationships that are interdependent. Links between countries can be transformed from confrontation to interdependence. The weakening of the core of a nation's industry is simply a shift of manufacturing to the most suitable location on an international scale. As far as Japan is concerned, this shift should result in its industries achieving greater technological advances.

Pushing this train of thought further, when economic interdependence grows, companies become multinational, and the world becomes increasingly borderless. The concept of national boundaries loses meaning. The fear that a nation's industrial core will weaken appears to spring from the idea that a full set of industries must exist in one country, although the history and underpinning of that single country are insignificant when compared with a broader view of humanity or religion.

If a country is to have a complete gamut of strong industries, it will be burdened with some that are internationally inefficient. Protecting the 'lame ducks' is expensive, and can cause friction with other countries. This must be what is happening in the world, and especially in Japan.

Interference by governments

Governments everywhere are increasingly interfering in the affairs of business. The result is that the role of government is becoming unnecessarily great, and government ministers seem to be continually involved in crisis management. Presently, it is the existence of national boundaries that makes economic problems become political ones. I believe that national boundaries prevent free competition and stop the natural flow toward equal economic specialization. They also inhibit efforts to achieve economic efficiency on a world scale.

Should one regard the changes occurring in Japan's economic structure as a weakening of the nation's industrial core? What can Japan expect from increasing global, and more specifically Asian, economic prosperity?

Would you say that, in the future, the world will become increasingly borderless? And, if it does, will the EU and NAFTA experiments succeed and would they serve as a good model for a borderless world?

September 21, 1994

There is no need for pessimism over the Japanese economy. The fear of 'hollowing out' rests on fallacies
Peter Drucker

Japan flies not on 'one wing', but on 'two wings'

Ten years ago, one of my main concerns was the over-dependence of Japan on the West. Then, two-fifths – a full 40 per cent – of all Japanese exports went to the United States, with another ten or fifteen per cent going to Europe. This was clearly over-dependence, and bound to provoke severe protectionist reaction in both the USA and Europe.

During the last ten years, Japan has restored the balance. Now its dependence on the West is down to less than one-third, or perhaps even to less than one-quarter. The US now accounts for less than one-fifth of Japan's exports. Mainland Asia, by contrast, now takes more in the way of Japanese goods than does the United States. Just as trade across the Pacific has become more important for the US in the last ten years than trade across the Atlantic – which is probably the major economic achievement of the United States during the last ten years, the years during which it all but doubled exports across the Pacific – trade across the Sea of Japan with mainland Asia now accounts for more of Japan's exports than trade across the Pacific to the US, and for almost as much trade with the entire West taken together. This, to repeat, is a tremendous achievement, and may be Japan's major recent economic achievement. Ten years ago, to use American slang, Japan tried to fly on one wing. Now Japan flies on two wings.

But this also means that Japan has a very high stake in the development of China.

Baseless pessimism over the Japanese economy

This leads to my appraising Japan's performance over the last ten years. In Japan itself, there is pessimism. From the outside, however, I see little reason for this. Japan's performance in becoming the leader in the development of mainland Asia is outstanding and practically unprecedented. At the same time, Japan has maintained its market standing in the United States, though the competition there is becoming increasingly intense. Japan has also greatly strengthened its position in Europe, despite tremendous protectionist resistance.

Services as a growth sector

Internally, the developments may be even more important. Japan's great weakness – and it is still so – is in the services sector. And this should be the lead growth sector of a developed economy. In the single most important growth area of a modern economy, finance, Japan, is, bluntly speaking, mired in inefficiency, over-control by a bureaucracy which does not understand modern finance, in over-staffing, and in the fatal tendency to substitute spending money on computers for thinking. This is something that we in the United States also did twenty or thirty years ago, but have since learned not to do any more.

Great work in the retail business

The shining exception is in the retail sector. I consider the achievements of Daiei, Ito-Yokado, and similar companies to be the most important achievement of the last ten years, in any of the developed countries.

When I first came to Japan, almost forty years ago, retailing in Japan was one of the greatest weaknesses. Japanese retailing then was stuck in the early Meiji era. The typical department store, the 'departo', was magnificent, but even then it had become dear that department stores were not the 'wave of the future.' Then there was the totally inefficient retail system of 'Mom-and-Pop stores' which, however, fulfilled an essential social function. In a country without unemployment insurance, this was the social safety net. Japan, on the one hand, had to develop modern retail distribution to be competitive. On the other hand, the totally inefficient retail sector was a social necessity.

In many ways, Japanese economic policy which is now so severely criticized – and not only in the West, but in Japan as well – was an attempt to make possible the conversion of a primitive retail trade into a modern distribution system without social upheaval. We all knew, thirty or forty years ago, that this had to be done, but nobody knew how it could possibly be done.

The reality today is that it has been done, and most successfully, by the new retailers. Their mechanism, which nobody could have possibly predicted, was to convert the Mom-and-Pop store of yesterday into the franchisee of a modern retail operation, fully-computerized, fully-automated, totally-controlled, and highly efficient – yet maintaining the old retailers, and with them the convenience and quality of retailing which is so important to Japanese customers. I consider this, easily, the greatest social achievement in any country of the last forty years.

Now, of course, the great challenge is to extend this to the other service areas, and especially to finance.

Finance as the high-tech frontier

Finance is probably the most challenging growth industry in the world today. It is a real high-tech frontier, not the finance of yesterday. And it has new challenges: to serve the rising class of affluent, though not rich, investors, especially those getting older; in the management of foreign exchange exposure; in asset management; in financing transnational business. Japanese financial institutions are not yet fully capable of competing in these markets.

What is needed, for instance, is the development of the kind of institution that can serve a totally different retail finance market. This market does not need speculative financial gains. It has to provide financial peace of mind to a rapidly-aging population, in which the greatest need is to make provision for living too long and thereby outliving one's financial resources, including one's pension.

There are thus real challenges in the Japanese economy, and they are in the services sector. Even in Japan, this is by far the biggest part of the economy. In fact, by the year 2000, the manufacturing sector will employ a small fraction of the total working population – probably no more than about one-sixth – where today it still employs one-third or more.

Fallacies about 'hollowing out'

This brings me to the question about the 'hollowing out' of Japanese manufacturing industry. You ask whether a country needs a strong manufacturing base to be a leading and strong economy. The answer is clearly, 'Yes,' but it does not need a large manufacturing work-force to have a strong manufacturing base.

What prompted the question was the concern in Japan that, by moving manufacturing work abroad, the country weakens its manufacturing base, which is the fear that underlies the catch-phrase 'hollowing out.' But this fear rests on four fallacies. In fact, moving out manufacturing work to places like mainland China or Thailand actually strengthens Japan's manufacturing base. There are four arguments for this.

1. The separation of production and employment

First, manufacturing production is not the same as manufacturing employment. Politicians, economists, journalists, the public at large are all convinced that manufacturing production and manufacturing employment are actually one and the same thing. Nothing could be further from the truth. It might even be said that with smaller manufacturing employment, manufacturing production is likely to be stronger and greater.

We have seen something like this in agriculture. At the end of the Pacific War, the United States still had more than one-quarter of its population working on the land as farmers. Today, the farm population accounts for no more than three percent of the US working population, yet farming production is seven times what it was in 1950. In Japan, similarly, farm population on the land was sixty percent at the end of the Pacific War, and not much lower than that in 1950. Today, it is down to a few percent, and very few of them are full-time farmers. Nevertheless, Japanese farm production remains at least as great as it was then.

In the US thirty years ago, making and moving things – in the factory, on the farm, in mining, in transportation – employed almost half the labor force. Today, moving and making things employs around a fifth of the labor force, with manufacturing employing no more than fifteen per cent – it was thirty-five per cent thirty or forty years ago. Yet American manufacturing production has grown as fast as the country's Gross National Product, or a little faster, and it has grown just as fast as Japanese production over the last fifteen years. It is now two and a half times what it was in 1980. Since then the employment of blue-collar manual workers in manufacturing has been cut by almost half.

Instead of automation

The cause of this was not 'automation'. On the contrary, the companies that tried to become competitive by investing huge amounts of money in automation lost ground, lost market share, lost competitiveness almost without exception. The best example is General Motors, still the world's largest manufacturing company, and still by far the world's largest automobile manufacturer. General Motors, in the early 1980s, had about as much money as Toyota has now. That means it had far more money than it needed in its own business. It invested practically all of it, a full thirty billion dollars, in automating its plants. The result was that costs went up, productivity and quality went down, and General Motors steadily lost market standing, not only to the Japanese, but even more to its American competitors, Ford and Chrysler. General Motors committed the worst sin a business can commit: it substituted money for thinking.

Toyota, even though it had the money, did not invest much in automation. Ford did not have the money to invest. Both companies instead invested a lot of thinking in manufacturing. They revolutionized the manufacturing process in the automotive industry. As a result, these two – and perhaps Nissan's plant in the Midlands of England should be included in this group as well – are now the most productive, and the most efficient automobile manufacturers in the world, with Toyota's US plants perhaps even more efficient than its Japanese plants. Toyota, Ford and Nissan spent an enormous amount of time and hard work on re-thinking their basic manufacturing process, and on re-engineering it around information and team work, rather than around machinery.

Transition in manufacturing

In other words, we are in the middle of a total re-think of manufacturing, in which blue-collar, industrial labor is being replaced by knowledge and information. A high labor coeffi-

cient in manufacturing production is actually a sign of obso-
lescence. No manufacturing operation, by the year 2000, can
hope to be competitive if its blue-collar, direct labor costs are
more than ten or twelve per cent. And this means that blue-
collar manufacturing labor in developed countries will not be
very much larger, as a proportion of the total work-force,
than the farm population is today – and yet, as in farming,
manufacturing will produce much more.

In that respect, the United States has essentially completed
the transition, or is close to it. In Japan, the majority of industries still have to start on the transition. What is predictable is that in the next few years blue-collar manufacturing
labor in Japan will shrink, perhaps not quite as fast as in the
US but certainly, eventually quite as far. At the same time,
manufacturing production will continue to rise, and swiftly.

2. The influence of a weak dollar on the Japanese economy

The second fallacy – and here I know that I am going to say
some very controversial things – is that Japan is being harmed
by the low dollar.

Individual companies that are heavily dependent for their
profits on exports to the United States certainly face problems if the dollar declines against the yen. But the last few
years have shown clearly that Japan as an economy and as a
competitor is helped rather than hindered by a weak dollar.
Even though the dollar today, against the yen, is down to 40
per cent of what it was only a few years ago – and to less than
a third of what it was twenty years ago – Japan's exports are
booming, including its exports to the United States.

The trade surplus continues to grow and grow. This could
not possibly have happened if a low dollar really harmed
Japan.

The explanation of the apparent paradox is that Japan actually spends more dollars abroad than it takes in abroad. If the
dollar goes down, Japan therefore benefits.

Dollar value and trade

Japan is the world's largest importer of food and raw materials, and of commodities as a whole. No other major country,
for instance, imports today 40 per cent of its food, let alone
all its petroleum, all its ores, and practically all its timber. All
commodities are priced in dollars. Contrary to what economic

theory would have predicted, the lower dollar did not result in higher commodity prices. On the contrary, commodity prices either stayed where they were, or went down even further. As an importer, in other words, Japan benefits tremendously by a low dollar. As an exporter, a very large part of Japan's exports, perhaps half of them, are not dependent on the dollar's value. They are the exports to Europe and to mainland Asia. The US, after all, now takes less than one-fifth of Japan's exports.

Conversely, the US clearly does not benefit from the low dollar, contrary to what the American government (and many economists) believe. For while Japan is the largest importer of commodities and foodstuffs, the US is still the world's largest exporter of them. Those exports are being penalized by the low dollar since their prices stay in dollars and do not go up if the dollar goes down. Individual Japanese companies, to repeat, suffer from the low dollar; individual American companies benefit from it. But the Japanese economy, overall, does not suffer from the low dollar and may benefit from it, while the US economy as a whole may not benefit from the low dollar, but may suffer from it.

3. Investment overseas and exports

The third fallacy is that moving production overseas leads to a decline in exports. Almost always, it leads in practice to a substantial increase in exports.

The Japanese manufacturer of automobiles or of consumer electronics who establishes a plant in a low wage country, perhaps Indonesia, may cut jobs in his own Japanese plant, though not many have done actually so. But the plant he builds in Indonesia will almost invariably be built by a Japanese construction company. The machines to be installed in this new plant invariably come from the same companies that have supplied the Japanese company in Japan, that is, from Japanese machine tool companies. Companies building new plants, whether at home or abroad, of necessity rely on their traditional suppliers. They are the people whose machines they have used for years; they are familiar, and can be depended upon. These also are relationships that have been built over many years. In new plants, except in the very lightest of industries such as knitting or making sneakers, the investment per worker in building equipment and machinery is, as a rule, equivalent to the worker's output over five years. In other words, new plants turn over their fixed capital once every five years. During these five years, the money spent on exports from Japan to the Indonesian plant – exports of machinery and payments to architects, for construction, and so on – exceeds what would have been spent in wages in Japan by a factor of five.

This, and this alone, explains the actual performance of Japan in the world economy in the last few years. It also explains the performance in the world economy of the United States in the 1960s and 1970s, when America 'exported jobs' that is, established jobs overseas. These were the years in which American trade surpluses grew rather than shrank. The explanation was simple: investment overseas creates exports. And it creates exports of goods of higher value than the ones which are being replaced. It creates exports for goods made by machine tool makers with high-skill and high-value-added to replace production by low-skill and low-value-added clothing workers or toy workers.

Creating new markets in developing countries

In addition, the belief that the output of these new plants actually replaces output of the plants at home, and will be imported back to the developed country (whether Japan or the US), is at best a partial truth. At first, it may indeed be true – as it was for the Japanese consumer electronics industry five or six years ago, when Sony and Matsushita first moved plants to low-wage counties. But within a very short time, say three to five years, these plants increasingly supply their own local markets. They create new markets rather than replace production in the old market of their own country.

In other words, there is abundant evidence – the figures are alone sufficient – that moving out low-wage and low-value-added manufacturing operations strengthen the manufacturing base of a developed country rather than 'hollows it out'.

4. The competitive advantage of low-wage countries

The final fallacy: low-wage countries have a competitive edge. Yes, low-wage countries can today very rapidly become as productive as high-wage countries. In the nineteenth century, and even as late as 1950, it was generally true that low-wage countries also had low productivity. It was then an axiom that productivity across the world was much the same everywhere: high in high-wage countries and low in low-wage countries. Then came a short period, after World War II, during which low-wage countries did have an advantage. They had learned how to train. This made it possible for countries like Japan in the 1950s and 1960s, and Korea ten years later, to gain considerable competitive advantage in the world economy for a few years, by having labor which, while still on lower wages, had the productivity of high-wage countries and therefore could compete easily with them and could underbid them.

The reducing importance of wage competition

This is no longer true for a very simple reason. Wages are no longer such an important factor in most manufacturing work. As long as workers' wages were forty per cent of operating costs, as they generally were only thirty years ago, wage competition was important and often decisive. In a developed economy like that of Japan or the United States, manufacturing operations in which direct blue-collar labor costs are more than twenty per cent of operating costs are, however, becoming increasingly the exception. They are, in fact, inefficient and obsolete, and need to be re-engineered. The process has gone perhaps furthest in the American steel industry where labor costs were almost forty per cent as recently as 1970, but are now below twenty per cent in all but the oldest and most inefficient plants.

In most manufacturing work, and in all the new industries, direct manufacturing labor costs are now well below twenty per cent. In most of them, they are well below fifteen per cent. Once direct labor costs go down to twelve per cent, low-wage labor simply no longer has a competitive edge. What one can save by paying lower wages one loses, even if the productivity of the low-wage labor is high. Freight to Japan from a country like Indonesia accounts by itself for five to seven percent of the value of most merchandise. There are quality problems, there are people problems. In other words, it is no longer possible for a developing country to compete in the world market on the basis of low-wage labor, at least not for many products.

Changes in US businesses

In fact, in the United States, more and more businesses are bringing home operations which, twenty or thirty years ago, they moved to low-wage countries. The share of direct labor in total costs has become too small to make a difference. We are moving back even operations with a high labor content, such as textiles or shoe-making, into plants in the United States. The labor cost differential no longer justifies their being so far removed from their markets.

Moving production offshore, in other words, should be seen primarily, and especially by businessmen, as a way to establish themselves in offshore markets rather than as a way to supply their own domestic market. And this is what is actually happening in Japan as well as in the US.

An empty theory of politicians in the United States

In fact, the belief in the US, and especially among labor union leaders and politicians, that low labor cost production overseas accounts for America's trade deficit is totally unfounded. America now imports about twelve per cent of the manufactured goods it consumes – still only half of what most European countries import. Hardly any of these imported manufactured goods come from low-wage countries. The American merchandise trade deficit, insofar as it is not caused by petroleum which accounts for almost half of it, is caused by such imports as automobiles and consumer electronics from Japan, and of machine tools of all kinds from Japan and Germany, that is, by imports from countries in which wages are higher than they are in the US, rather than lower. Only three per cent of America's consumption is supplied by imports from low-wage countries. And only half of that consists of imports of manufactured goods from low-wage countries such as mainland China. These imports, precisely because they are simple consumer goods such as sneakers or toys, are very visible in our retail stores. In the total American economy they play almost no role and have nothing to do with America's economic problems. The same, it can confidently be predicted, will be the case in Japan.

A big problem – dislocation of the work force

There is, however, a problem: dislocation. Total employment in the country that moves out production is going to go up, as it did in the United States. But the people who get the new jobs are not the same people as those who lose the old ones. The shift away from farming between 1950 and 1990 – that is, the shift from a society in which in practically every country (Great Britain and Belgium being the main exceptions) farming employed by far the largest portion of the labor force, to today, where employment in farming is minimal – created no dislocation. The new jobs in the in mass-production plants offered better pay and easier work than did farming. Even a poor farmer had the skills needed to become a productive and well-paid worker in a mass-production plant.

Today the shift is from relatively low-skilled mass-production jobs to jobs in high engineering or high-tech industries, where the pay is considerably better (at least in the US, and also in Japan), but where the requirement for skill and education are very much higher. Even if he has a high school education, as the Japanese worker by now commonly has, the mass-production worker is not, as a rule, educated to be a technologist.

What will matter even more in Japan is that the new jobs are not in the plants, the companies, and the industries where the old ones were. The transition thus threatens employment security.

The responsibility of employers

There is a need, I would assert, to maintain the basic principles on which so much of Japan's growth in the last forty years has been based. The principle, first, of employment stability, even though there is unlikely still to be lifetime employment for large numbers of people twenty years hence. The second principle which I consider perhaps equally important is the essential identity of interests between company and employee, or at least the harmony of their interests. This, I would say, requires active policies on the part of employers, especially of large employers. It requires that the employer asserts his concern and his responsibility. It requires active and energetic attempts at retraining for specific new job opportunities. It requires that the employer takes responsibility for placing redundant employees in new jobs. These are things which I am advocating for the United States too. Quite a few American employers accept these responsibilities, which explains why the tremendous shift in our work force in the last twenty years has created practically no social unrest. I think such employer responsibility for dislocation is particularly important in Japan, with its strong belief in social harmony and mutual obligation.

November 10, 1994

Developing countries don't need government-to-government aid, but partnerships with private enterprises in developed nations
Peter Drucker

Failure in development aid

Taking up the role of Japan in the economic development of Asia, and in the world at large, may I begin with my own personal experiences. I was one of the earliest advocates of development aid. Indeed, I may claim to have been one of the first people to speak of it, way back in the 1940s and early 1950s, when I was a consultant to the first two presidents of the World Bank. I was also active in those years in development aid policies, for example the American Marshall Plan for the recovery of a war-devastated Europe. I was an enthusiastic supporter of President Truman's 'Point Four,' which made development aid part of America's official policy, the first country to do so. I was equally an enthusiastic supporter of President Kennedy's 'Alliance for Progress' for development aid to Latin America, and did a considerable amount of work for the 'Alliance for Progress' in the 1960's.

But I have become totally disillusioned. I have learned that government-to-government aid does not work. We know the reasons for it. We know that government-to-government aid – and the World Bank, in this respect, is a governmental institution – often becomes military aid, which is then wasted on useless arms, as so much of US aid to South America has been. Or, it goes to enrich governments and government bureaucrats. Or worst, perhaps it is wasted on grandiose projects in countries which do not have the resources or the markets for them. This has been the fate of so much World Bank aid.

What has worked, however, and has worked exceedingly well, is development based on the private sector. The countries that have developed most in the last fifty years have developed either totally without development aid, like Japan, or with a minimum of aid, as did Korea, and today, Mainland China.

Private sector initiative

Development is not a matter of money. It is a matter of human resource, developed by and through specific projects in which people from developed countries work closely with people from the developing countries. It is no accident that so many of the leading German companies are now being run by people who first worked for American companies investing in Germany, twenty or thirty years ago. It is no accident that so much of Japanese development came out of the joint ventures with American companies which transferred technology to Japan. It is no accident that Japan honors the memory of Dr Edwards Deming who worked on human competence and human responsibility. Thus, I see the role of Japan – or of any other developed country – in encouraging private enterprise to be active as partners in developing countries.

There are no 'underdeveloped' countries any more. There are only mis-managed countries, and management is not being created by government-to-government aid, by money at all. It is being created by example, by leadership, by giving responsibility, and this is best done by individual organizations; they repeat in a developing country what they do well in their own developed one.

I know that this is not a popular thing to say in Japan today. In many ways, people in Japan today believe in development aid the way we in the United States believed in it thirty years ago, when President Kennedy proclaimed the 'Alliance for Progress.' I only hope that in ten years time you will not come to the same conclusion that we have reached in the United States: government-to-government aid does not develop. It may not do much harm, but it does little good. It is private initiative, the leadership of people, the example of people, the development of the human resource in which a developed country can inspire and in which it can discharge its responsibility towards the developing world.

November 10, 1994

Management has to learn to balance the three dimensions – global, regional and local
Peter Drucker

The borderless world

In some ways, the world is indeed becoming borderless. Money and information no longer know borders. They have become transnational. Knowledge and technology have equally become more or less borderless, but, at the same time, we have seen a strong regional development. The new regions are basically protectionist. This is true for the EU and it is largely true for NAFTA. Then there is the strong tendency towards the breakup of large units and the creation of small, sometimes incredibly small, new nations. This is what has been happening in the former Soviet Union. It is now happening in Yugoslavia with tragic effects. Within ten years or so, Canada's Quebec may well be a separate nation within North America.

I no longer have to travel to address audiences in foreign countries. Within the last few months, I have spoken to very large audiences in Berlin, in São Paulo, and in Johannesburg, without traveling to Germany, Brazil, or South Africa. I have done so through video conferences and satellite communications. It is also perfectly true that every business in the world today needs information about the world economy. So far, very few companies have it, the large Japanese trading companies being among the few exceptions.

Localization

At the same time, it is also true that you increasingly have to conduct research where the experts are. If you want to research in veterinary medicine, you need to do it in France, for France has the best specialists in this field. They are not willing to move to Tsukuba or to the United States. They prefer to stay in France. Many Japanese computer manufacturers have bought minority interests in Silicon Valley companies to gain access to specialized knowledge. Again, very few Silicon Valley people would be willing to move to Tsukuba. Two large Japanese companies have become very strong in the American food retailing business. Yamazaki Bakery owns and runs a number of successful bakeries in the United States, and Ito-Yokado owns and runs America's Seven-Eleven stores. But the Yamazaki-owned bakeries in the US are being run as

American businesses, and the breads they bake are designed for American tastes. Ito-Yokado runs its Seven-Eleven stores as American stores.

EU and NAFTA

Neither the European Union nor NAFTA have created 'borderless' regions. To be sure, goods in Europe can now move easily, and so can people, but no more than they did before 1914. Capital movements are still quite limited. The only companies in Europe that have become truly 'European' companies are either those domiciled in small counties like Switzerland or Holland – that is, companies who have been European for a hundred years or longer – or they are companies from outside Europe, especially the American companies in Europe, and increasingly, the Japanese companies.

European companies have generally become more rather than less national. The big banks in Europe are trying to become the dominant banks in their own nations by merger with smaller banks within their own country. Not one of these big banks has tried to become a European bank so far. And the same is true of most manufacturing companies.

Globalized top management

To do business in the world today, even within one's own national boundaries requires 'thinking globally,' and any business that operates beyond its own national boundaries will have to make one radical change: it will have to build a transnational top management in which people of different nationalities, with different background and different experiences, work together as a team. There are already a few examples. One is Nestlé, the Switzerland-based processed-foods company. In its top management, a half-dozen different nationalities are represented. There is Coca-Cola and other food processors in the US, and there is Citibank in the financial field. These, so far, are the exceptions. To build such a management is clearly a major task, and it is difficult. How difficult is shown by the troubled relationships between the large Japanese consumer electronics companies, like Sony and Matsushita, and their American 'software' subsidiaries, the movie and program producers in Hollywood. Even where there are no cultural differences at all, to build transnational management has not been proven easy for anybody. There is one company today that has a truly European management. It is the European subsidiary of the (American) Ford Motor

Company. Americans, Englishmen, Germans, Italians, and Frenchmen work together there in a common top-management team. But it took the Ford Motor Company twenty years of very hard work to develop this team.

Regional integration in today's world

Neither the European Union nor NAFTA can really serve as examples. I would describe neither as 'borderless,' and other regional blocs will certainly have to develop their own rules, their own principles, their own ways of integration. The integration of the region that is now emerging in Latin America should have been fairly simple. After all, in Mercosur – the regional economy which makes Argentina, Brazil, Paraguay and Uruguay 'borderless' – there is a great deal of cultural unity. Even there, the Brazilians, and the Argentineans, and the Paraguayan have found it exceedingly difficult to go beyond their own borders except for the exchange of goods. They all maintain their own laws, as do the countries of the European Union and NAFTA. They maintain their own financial regulations, and their own taxation systems. In other words, what you have is a free-trade zone rather than an economic union. As I already said, this was the norm before 1914, worldwide. There were, for instance, no tariffs within the entire British Empire.

Regionalization in Asia

The most important emerging regions will not be able to follow the example of others. These are the regions of Asia, and no-one can know how many regions tomorrow's Mainland Asia will have. Coastal China by itself is certainly big enough to be a region of its own, and distinct enough. South East Asia and the ASEAN countries together, are also big enough to be a region, but, unlike Coastal China, they are extremely diverse – culturally, socially, and politically. Half, for instance, have a Confucian tradition; the other half are Muslim. The relationship of Japan to either of those two regions still has to be worked out and cannot even be guessed at.

Globalization, regionalization and localization

In other words, managements increasingly will have to learn to operate in three dimensions, and to balance the three. They will have to learn to operate in the world economy. Their own market may be purely local, but competition is already world-wide. They will, in many cases, have to learn to operate regionally, and each region is bound to be quite different from any other. The market may in many ways become more local, in its requirements, in its tastes and preferences, in its buying habits, than it has ever been before. This, I think, is one of the greatest challenges facing managements, especially the managements of large companies – manufacturing companies as well as banks, probably retailers as well, and perhaps also universities. The key may well be the ability to build a management team that goes beyond any one nationality and yet is united in its dedication to the welfare of the company, the welfare of its employees, and the satisfaction of its customers. This may well be the biggest management challenge facing us in the next twenty-five years.

Challenges for executives

My dear Mr Nakauchi, I hope that I have been able to answer your questions. I also hope that I have been able to raise new questions. For I do not believe that any one of your questions can really be answered. What makes them so important and so stimulating is that they are precisely focused on the challenges we are facing in the next ten years. I can try to give answers, but the answers will in effect be given by business leaders and business executives, and primarily by business leaders and business executives in the developed countries such as yours and mine. All I can hope is that these answers of mine will stimulate enough of the business executives to think through their own roles, their own opportunities, and their own strategies.

What my so-called answers really do is to ask the business executive in Japan: What do these things mean to you? What opportunities do they offer to you? What responsibilities do they impose on you?

November 10, 1994

Knowledge plays an important role in changing industrial structures
Isao Nakauchi

'Hollowing out' and changing industrial structure

One of the many responsibilities of Japanese business executives that you mentioned was the need to address the so-called 'hollowing out' of Japanese industry. I was very consoled to hear your view that fears of hollowing out are founded on a misunderstanding.

Although changing the industrial structure in Japan represents a task of the utmost urgency, the need for this change is not properly understood, even within industrial circles. I believe that many in Japan would be convinced of the need for change by the clear explanation in your reply. You emphatically refuted the idea that an increase in overseas operation by manufacturers represents weakening of domestic industrial fundamentals, arguing that the transfer of unproductive manufacturing operations overseas serves to strengthen manufacturing industries in developed countries.

Redesigning business

Mentioning the American and Japanese automobile manufacturers Toyota, Ford and Nissan, you indicated that the experience of these companies demonstrates that success in manufacturing industries is achieved through fundamental business redesign, by converting manual laborers in the factories into sources of knowledge and information, rather than by enormous investments in automation plant.

In my experience, such business redesign is equally applicable and effective in non-manufacturing industries, and especially in the retail sector.

Modernization of the retail industry in Japan has been underway for some twenty years, with the conversion of inefficient, family-run businesses into modern convenience store chains through franchising. This fundamental redesign has benefited consumers by maintaining many small retail outlets, while simultaneously boosting productivity in the industry through modernization, without the need for massive investment. I should note at this stage that the concept of franchising was, of course, borrowed from the United States.

Convenience store chains

The first outlet in the Lawson franchise convenience store chain which is affiliated to Daiei opened in 1975. In the following twenty years we established over 5,000 outlets. Today the existence of convenience stores is an indispensable part of life to all Japanese, men and women, young or old. Computerized POS systems put convenience stores at the leading edge of the Japanese retail industry. For this reason, it is often said that computer technology modernized the network of convenience stores. My experience tells me, however, that the franchising approach itself, and the wealth of related information it brings, are of far greater significance.

The concept of franchising proceeds as follows. Where possible, duplicate work should be avoided. Each element is important: store design, shelf layout, establishing logistics systems for purchasing and delivery, drawing up rules for store management and part time workers, and compiling sales figures for distribution to retail outlets and manufacturers. Simultaneously, the independence of store owners must be preserved to bring them satisfaction from managing their own business. Finally it is of vital importance to secure the best locations convenient to consumers, and to offer a variety of items. Such a franchising concept was the driving force behind the conversion of retail outlets from family-run businesses into modern convenience stores. Computers and POS systems, while important, are no more than tools. Conceptualization and decision-making by people are always more important than utilization of the range of tools that support management.

Franchising systems apply not just to convenience stores and other retail outlets, but also to eating and drinking establishments. At Daiei, we employ franchising systems in discount stores, with slightly larger floor area than convenience stores, and in fast-food outlets serving hamburgers or local specialities.

Thus, knowledge is the key in changing the industrial structure in Japan. There is no longer any doubt that Japan must strive to become a knowledge society, as you have suggested for some time.

Supporting the development of human resources

Your reply to my question regarding the role of Japan with respect to Asia and other developing countries also touched on this point. Your description of a role of Japan and other industrialized countries as providers of private-sector initiative and leadership, in setting examples and providing support for human resource development, really boils down to an exchange of knowledge. I would like to suggest that the way to get started is to exchange knowledge on a global scale.

Problems of regionalism

We are currently witnessing the advent of regionalism in many parts of the world. Despite strenuous claims by EU and NAFTA to the contrary, this inevitably gives rise to doubts by outsiders about the emergence of closed economic spheres. I totally agree with your reply on this point. The claim that the rise of regionalism is directly linked to economic blocs may turn out to be nonsense. I can understand the point made by proponents of regionalism who argue that liberalization within designated regions will subsequently spread throughout the world.

The question is one of timing: while liberalization proceeds within a designated region, the pace of economic progress outside it may be slowing, before the expected spillover can provide benefit. The European Union began with the establishment in 1957 of the European Economic Community. It took more than 30 years to achieve the Maastricht Treaty establishing the European Union. In 1957 Japan was poised to enter the period of postwar rapid economic growth. At that time, no-one could possibly have foretold that Japan would become a leading player in the world economy, that oil crises would force the world to accept the scarcity of its basic natural resources, the collapse of the Berlin Wall, nor the subsequent demise of the Soviet Union, all as predicted in your work *The New Realities*. In the same way, one cannot accept unreservedly the argument that regionalism will become the rule in the future global economy. The world is now confronted with global environmental issues that extend beyond the scarcity of natural resources and threaten to affect the very future of humankind. We have no time to lose.

Japan has been assigned a role of global importance. Generous foreign countries shared their resources and that helped mineral-poor Japan to prosper. Looking at the seriousness of global environmental problems, I firmly believe that what is expected of Japan must be performed in full. It is imperative that we start examining ways to utilize resources effectively from the global perspective. It is now time for economic liberalization on a global scale, rather than within blocs. Through this, we must find the most effective methods of production and take a borderless, global perspective in determining the optimum location for industries and companies. We must realize that this is not a role for governments, operating as they do primarily in terms of national boundaries. It is the duty of private industry.

I believe that Japanese entrepreneurs should be more aware of their responsibilities in this regard. Instead of casting across the globe in search of cheap land and cheap labor, it is necessary to make a firm commitment to the local community and then build up operations in line with local requirements, passing on management knowledge and skills without reserve, developing potential human resources and contributing to global growth. My decision to invest in China exemplifies this approach. The concept of thinking globally and acting locally requires local initiatives of this kind throughout the world.

The responsibility of employment

You also mentioned the importance of developing human resources as an executive responsibility, a fact almost forgotten by a Japanese business community shivering before the word 'recession'.

Some say that, in the future, Japanese companies will no longer require workers unfamiliar with computers, since simple tasks will have been transferred to less expensive workers overseas. There is some truth to this argument. The importance of computers in business is already widely accepted. The information revolution, which has spread to Japan from the United States and Europe, is fueling the progress of information technology that has engulfed Asia. One may say that the importance of multimedia as a business tool can only increase from here on. In view of my responsibilities as an entrepreneur, however, I cannot agree with this approach, which completely ignores the importance of human resources. Sadly, the proponents of this argument today are the same Japanese business managers and scholars who several years ago were espousing Japanese-style management and its emphasis on human resources. I believe it is quite wrong to dismiss the matter in this way.

The private sector in Japan must work to improve productivity if it is to weather the vicissitudes of the world economy. Mobility in the labor market must rise, and life-long employment schemes as well as age-based salary scales must face change. For that purpose measures are required to improve mobility, to minimize labor mismatches such as manufacturing against services, urban against rural, and young against old.

As you point out, the key to improvement lies in the capacity of businesses to adopt a borderless perspective and to form management teams wholly devoted to the task of bringing profits to the business and to employees, and satisfaction to customers. At this crucial time, with the Japanese economy poised at a major turning point, it is unacceptable for responsible managers to make statements that discount the past contributions (both large and small) of workers to their enterprises. Naturally, the self-responsibility of employees must also be examined. Now, more than ever, it is vital that employees make their own decisions about the skills they need in order to contribute to their companies, to society, and to the world.

Nevertheless, it is impossible to lay all the burden on employees. In your essay 'Can There Be Business Ethics' in *The Future Which Already Happened,* the traditional Confucian concept of mutual responsibility is clearly stated. I believe that those managers who are aware of the extent of their responsibility for employees must now strive to create mutual recognition, so that all employees can perform to their best ability based on an understanding of their responsibilities.

The importance of education

This will require a fundamental reappraisal of current hiring and training practices that are predicated on the lifelong employment system. Unfortunately, Japanese education is geared toward achieving entry into top-ranking universities in order to guarantee subsequent entry into top-ranking enterprises, as you pointed out in 'A View of Japan Through Japanese Art,' again in *The Future Which Already Happened.* Such an education system is incapable of fostering the human resources necessary for the future of Japan.

As a long standing member of the National Council on Education Reform, I have often argued for the need to emphasize individuality. I believe that what is needed today is education centered on this very concept. Emphasis on individuality is often linked too simplistically to the acquisition of specialized skills by those who argue for more specialization in university courses and more practical education to achieve immediate effects. While this may be true to some extent, of still greater importance is to understand that such knowledge will quickly lose relevance in a rapidly changing society. In this sense, it is important to pursue the post-graduation learning process.

Universities should serve as places for personal reflection on future aims and the skills needed to contribute to society. Their roles should not be limited only to practical and businesslike education. One must bear in his mind that such personal reflection should continue beyond institutional education. This means that university should serve as a place for self-development, rather than just a place for learning. Specifically, Japanese universities need to place greater emphasis on this self-development aspect. Off-campus programs, recurrent systems, and other schemes can prepare young people for economic and social change.

Similarly, private enterprises should view universities not as sources of workers but as places to be used actively for employee re-education. Again, the exchange of knowledge represents an important aspect. Enterprises could provide up-to-date information on the world economy to universities, which could in turn use such information to research constant factors and the direction of underlying trends. I believe that this type of continual interdependence is vital.

I established the University of Marketing and Distribution Sciences to put these concepts into practice. The University's aim combines practical business education with progressive study into knowledge exchanges between private industry and universities. Against considerable odds, we have struggled to shed light on what you once called the Dark Continent of distribution.

I feel it is important for private enterprise to contribute actively in this way to the development of employee re-education systems, in turn gradually reforming the entire Japanese education system.

Developing one's strength

As you pointed out at a recent seminar in Tokyo, it is the responsibility of every one of us to develop our strength. You also argued that this extends to executive responsibility for

49

corporate restructuring and personnel cutbacks. Listening to your address, I realized that, in preparation for the advent of the knowledge society, the role of corporations is to assist employees' efforts to optimize their strength. This will give corporations the capacity to contribute to the well-being of society, while transforming them into aggregations of individuals with a strong will for self-improvement. As economies become more integrated globally, Japanese corporations increasingly must think globally and act locally. Human resource development will be as important overseas as at home. Executives must possess a *global* sense of responsibility.

Professor Drucker, your stern letter has encouraged me to reappraise the duty of executives in the knowledge society, as opposed to the tendency of inward-looking Japanese managers who are casting about for the best way to cut excess staff during this prolonged recession.

December 7, 1994

3

The challenges of the 'knowledge society'

Present educational systems cannot develop talent for the 'knowledge society'
Isao Nakauchi

I WOULD LIKE TO ASK SOME QUESTIONS designed to enable me and other Japanese executives to reappraise the importance of our responsibilities.

There is no longer any doubt that education will take on great significance for the transformation of Japan into a knowledge society. However, its present education system is centered on rote learning of facts, such as memorizing the results of chemical reactions, without any thought of the underlying process or experiment. Evidently such an educational system is incapable of developing the human resources, full of creativity and self-responsibility, required by a knowledge-based society. This system, persisting despite continuing and widespread misgivings, must be reformed. I would like to hear your thoughts on what an 'educated person' should be, equipped for the knowledge society. Your opinion will be valuable for the reform of education in Japan.

December 7, 1994

The Japanese educational system itself is not wrong. Japan has its own forms of creativity and originality
Peter Drucker

Problems imposed from outside the education system

I hope you will forgive me if I start out by saying that I have always found it very difficult to understand the criticism that you in Japan have of your educational system. To be sure, there are some very serious things wrong with it, but they are not, as far as I can see, the fault of the educational system. They have been imposed from the outside, and largely by events of the last thirty or forty years to which society has not yet adjusted.

I have been hearing for many years that the Japanese educational system breeds conformity, that it stifles originality and creativity, and creates organization-men who cannot make decisions, cannot innovate, cannot think for themselves. The results, my dear Mr Nakauchi, do not support these allegations. In fact, to an outsider such as me, the amazing fact is the tremendous amount of originality and creativity that has characterized Japan for many centuries.

Individuality in Japanese arts

As you know, I have been interested in Japanese art for more than sixty years. One of the things that attracted me to it – and still fascinates me – is the tremendous individuality of the Japanese artist. If you look at Western art, there is one prevailing style, one prevailing aesthetics at any one time. This has not been true of Japanese art since early Muromachi days. There have always been several, sometimes six or seven, different aesthetics and different styles existing side-by-side, with many artists working in more than one style and more than one aesthetic at the same time. Yet the young artist began to work in a school, and spent ten or fifteen years learning to be a master in that school. Then he blossomed forth into an artist on his own, with tremendous individuality. As I dictate this letter, sitting in my study, I look at three paintings produced by three different artists of the same school who lived at the same time, and who studied under the same masters. And each of the three paintings is strikingly different. At one glance one sees a different artist. In fact, this was the official philosophy of that great intellectual and artistic movement which I am convinced created modern Japan, the movement of the Bunjin of the late Edo period. Their creed was to enable each of the artists in each circle, or in each studio, to develop his own talent and capacities to the utmost - and they succeeded in a way that goes way beyond anything ever done in the West.

Individuality in Japanese company and university

This is still largely true today. I do not pretend to understand it, but it is a fact. There are those faceless, anonymous, organization-men in the Japanese company, who for the first twenty-five years of their career work as subordinates. Then, at age forty-five or so, they are appointed to senior positions. Suddenly, you have as large a number of individuals with their own policies, their own styles, their own strategies, as you have in any country in the world. You see that in the Japanese university. The way Japan treats young scholars in the universities always shocks us in the West. For twenty years they are treated as subordinates rather than as colleagues. They are not encouraged to do their own research – in fact, they do so at their peril. At age forty-five they finally get the full professorship. Then an amazing number of them become individuals, become pioneers in their discipline, and extremely original. Do not ask me to explain this. I know that it would not work in the West, but it works in Japan. I cannot, therefore, accept the criticism I hear in Japan all the time that the Japanese school system creates conformists and destroys individuality, originality, and initiative.

Experience within Japanese schools

My own experience within Japanese schools is quite different. I have visited quite a few elementary schools, over the years. The young children of friends of mine – then eight, nine or ten years old – invited me to come to their schools, some in Tokyo, some in Kyoto, some in Fukuoka. These were ordinary neighborhood schools, and not particularly distinguished ones, but I was impressed by the warmth of the class, by the mutual respect between teacher and students, also by the gaiety and freedom of the school. Those classes were lively. The children were disciplined, but they were not conformists. I also went to quite a few high schools, again as a guest either of a teacher or of a student. I found very much the same spirit there. It was above all the warmth of the relationship between teacher and student that so greatly impressed me. For a good many years, we spent weeks in the countryside of Japan climbing mountains, usually accompanied by two of our younger children. So, whenever we spent an evening at a camp site in a small town at the foot of a mountain, we would be invited to join a Japanese school class on its excursion. Again, I was tremendously impressed by the relationship between the teacher and the students, their warm friendship, their mutual respect; and their spontaneity. As far as I am concerned, the criticism which I hear in Japan all the time, mainly that your schools breed conformists and repress originality and individuality, does not agree with my own experiences and impressions.

Student against student

There are major problems, I admit. The pressure on the child in the Japanese school today to prepare for the 'examination hell' is extremely unhealthy. I think all of us agree on that. What bothers me the most is not that it deprives young people of their childhood, though it does that. What really bothers me is that it sets individual student against individual student. I was deeply shocked a few years back- when the son of a friend of ours, a fourteen year old, told me with great glee that his best friend was seriously sick and therefore would not be a competitor in the examination for high school entrance. Such an attitude would not be permitted in the West. We insist, especially in the United States, that the youngsters in a school see themselves as team-mates. In fact, our better schools are as much concerned with mutual support and with being a team player as the large Japanese corporations are in respect to young employees.

Leading universities and careers into the top echelon

Equally serious, at least to this foreign observer, is the fact that your present system deprives Japan of the full yield from a very large part of your human resources. It restricts careers, especially careers into the top echelon – in government, in the leading universities, and in major businesses – to the graduates of a few prestige universities. I am willing to admit, though I am not convinced at all, that these few universities may attract a disproportionate number of the ablest and brightest of the young people. All we know about the way human beings develop argues against the thesis that all young people develop at the same pace and rhythm and that, therefore, performance at age seventeen or eighteen is a reliable indication of ability and potential. Even if a very large proportion, make it fifty per cent, of the ablest and the brightest are the ones who are admitted to the prestige universities, that means that at least half of the pool of potential and ability in the Japanese population is kept out of top careers. No country can afford such a waste today. We need a system that reaches out and brings into productive work and contribution the largest possible proportion of ability and potential we can find in the nation.

Plutocracy in education

Increasingly, the Japanese educational system does not reward ability and potential. It rewards money. Increasingly, to get into the prestige universities requires a family that has the money to pay for the cram-school, and a family rich enough to give the young student a room of his or her own to study. Considering how small Japanese apartments usually are, this means that working class children, and even lower-middle class children, are increasingly unlikely to be able to afford prestige education, no matter how able they are. This is not meritocracy. This is plutocracy. And it bothers me a great deal.

Universities before World War II

All this is, however, most definitely not the fault of your educational system. The reason is that we have not adjusted to the changes of the last fifty years, and the same comment applies equally outside Japan. If you go back to the days when I was a high school student getting ready for the university, anybody in any European country could enter any university provided he or she had finished high school. This was not only true of Japan, it was true the world over. I attained my high school graduation in 1927, in Austria. I did not apply for admission to the university. I simply appeared with my diploma, and enrolled. I could have enrolled in any university in Europe, even though my diploma was an Austrian one. In fact, I had applied to Oxford, when I decided instead to go to Hamburg in Germany. I could just as well have gone to Sweden, or to Italy, or to Spain, or to France.

The same thing was true in the United States. When I first came to the United States in 1937, I soon got to know Princeton

University very well. Even then it was considered a high-prestige university, but if you had a high school diploma you were accepted in Princeton. In fact every year, when the University opened in September, a few young men appeared who had not applied at all. They presented their high school certificate and were admitted. In Japan, you had almost the same situation. There were more place in the Japanese prestige universities than there were students. And so, if you did a decent job in your high school, and if you could afford it, you were automatically admitted to whatever university you or your parents chose.

An explosion in university attendance

Then came the tremendous explosion of university attendance after World War II, which forced us into rigorous admissions procedures. On the European continent, anyone with a high school diploma is still automatically eligible for the university, but no longer for any university in Europe. If you graduate from an Austrian high school, you have to go to university in Austria. You can no longer go to Hamburg in Germany, as I did, sixty-eight years ago. You have the same pressures in Japan, but because you inherited a close relationship between employers and individual universities from pre-War days, the restrictions now create the pressures – pressures which underlie the cram-school, that underlie the 'examination hell', and which distort the entire educational system. The purpose is no longer to learn, but to have a career, and this is incompatible with education and with human development.

This approach deprives the nation of talent and ability. It is totally impossible, by any law of statistics, that the small proportion of young people who do well in formal examinations contain more than a small fraction of the ablest young people in the nation. The present system thus impoverishes the nation.

'Examination hell' and the desire to innovate

There is yet one more reason why the present system – with its enormous pressures on teenagers to cram for examinations – may do tremendous damage to Japan. Whenever we have made a study of successful innovators, especially in new fields such as information technology, genetics, material sciences and physics in general, and also in music or mathematics, or finance, we have found that these people start their interests while they are twelve or thirteen, and usually not much later than fourteen. Then they become enamored of their subject; they become amateurs. They spend endless hours doing experiments, reading, building models, and so on. Most of these young people are good students despite their absorption in a scientific or technical area which is outside the school and totally outside the curriculum, but they are rarely top students. Their main interests are outside of school. When these people reach their early twenties, what had been a hobby during their years, becomes a major career.

Constraining entrepreneurial spirit

The present Japanese system gives the young person no time to do anything except prepare for the next examination. It completely imposes school subjects on the teenager – and school subjects, by definition, deal with yesterday, deal with what is already known, and exclude experimentation, curiosity, and playing around.

I am not saying that most American young people spend the time our school system gives them on productive interests. On the contrary, most of them surely waste most of that free time. I myself, for instance, wasted endless hours as a teenager writing very poor poetry. The successful innovators of the last thirty years – and not only in such areas as computer design or software, but in most scientific and technical fields – trace the beginning of their interest to their middle school or at the latest, their high school years, almost without exception. As I will discuss later, we can build innovation into existing organizations. What we cannot do is to build the entrepreneurial spirit into an organization. That is a matter of the individual. You, for instance, certainly did not derive your desire to innovate, and your capacity to do so, from anything the organization did, but from your own inner drive. The present social climate in Japan (not the schools) militates against exactly that. If you indulge in outside interests, you are likely to fail the examination on school subjects and, thus, be deprived of access to a first-rate university and, ultimately, of access to a first-rate career. If you submit to the pressure and, as a result, make it into a first-rate university and into the first-rate career, your drive to innovate may have been destroyed. Our evidence strongly suggests that this drive has to be developed, preferably encouraged, in the teen years to become productive five or ten years later.

Improvement of the current situation

I think it is fairly easy to change the system, or at least to alleviate it to the point where its worst effects are eliminated. The major Japanese employers, both businesses and government, should recruit from twenty-five universities rather than from three or four. If they then treated all people, regardless of their university, the same way in respect to career and promotions, the worst effects of your system, I am convinced, would disappear within a few years – the examination hell, the cram-schools, and the terror and trauma inflicted on those who don't make it into Tokyo University or Keio University, and who therefore see themselves condemned at age eighteen to a lifetime of inferiority. Let me repeat that what I am talking about is not a weakness of the educational system. It is a weakness of society. It is not the result of anything that was designed intentionally. It is the result of pure accident – the post-War expansion of university attendance has not yet been reflected in the employment system. The employment system is still based on the realities of seventy-five years ago, and not on the realities of today.

Very similar problems are to be found in the systems of most other developed countries, though they are most pronounced in the Japan for the simple reason that no other nation demonstrates such a close relationship between individual universities and individual employers. This, in many ways, is a great strength, both of the Japanese university system and of Japanese society, but it has lead to the exclusion a very large fraction, perhaps a majority, of ability and potential from access to careers. It has became counter-productive and needs to be changed.

Japanese creativity and originality

Let me repeat again: this is something that has been inflicted on the system from the outside, rather than a fault of the Japanese educational system itself. I am sure that there are many faults in the Japanese educational system – true of school systems the world over – but the most commonly-heard complaint, that it creates conformity and stifles originality and creativity, I cannot accept. When I look at the final results, that is, at the performance of Japanese society and economy, and also at Japanese arts – architecture, literature, the woodblock print, music, theater, ceramics – I see more creativity and more originality than I see in any other country. Perhaps these results are achieved despite the school system, but there is no question in my mind that these are the results.

December 20, 1994

Continued learning is essential in the knowledge society. Wisdom is what being educated has always meant
Peter Drucker

Computers and education

Now let me turn to what we need tomorrow in schools and education. There is very little doubt that the school of the future will have to be very different from the school of the past, and from the school of today.

You rightly point out that the computer is only a tool, but tools do have an impact on their users. A new tool enables us to do old things in a new way, and this is certainly as true of the computer as it was of any earlier tool. A new tool also enables us to do new things we could not do before. A tool, one of the great biologists of the nineteenth century pointed out, is an extension of the human personality. It is purposeful, directed, man-made evolution. A new tool means that the user of the tool becomes different. This is certainly true of the new information technology. The institution on which the new information technology is likely to have the greatest impact is probably the school.

One reason for this is that the computer is so incredibly child-friendly. One only has to watch a nine-year old with a computer to realize that the computer responds to the child in ways no earlier tool and no earlier toy did. It has infinite patience. It adjusts itself completely to the speed and the rhythm of the user. It never says, 'You are stupid.' It is playful.

Separating learning and teaching

Above all, the computer enables us to separate learning and teaching. In the typical school, most of the time of the teacher

59

is not spent on teaching. It is spent on supervised learning, whether that of Japanese characters, or of multiplication, or of historical data. This, the computer does infinitely better and, by the way, much more cheaply. The computer is going to free the teacher to teach, that is, to work with the individual, and especially to work on the strengths of the individual. So far, wherever we have brought computers into the schools, the whole atmosphere has changed. Children are eager to learn, in fact more eager to learn than the school is usually prepared to let them learn. Teachers suddenly find themselves able to work with individual students on the student's individual projects and, especially, on the student's individual strengths.

Computers and the transformation of schools

The school of tomorrow, in other words, is going to be transformed by technology, even more than the business of tomorrow.

The last great transformation of the school in the West was brought about by the printed book, three hundred years ago. Japan accepted the printed book in the early Edo period. Then Japanese society took off, during the Tokugawa years, and created one of the world's greatest and most unique civilizations. The Chinese rejected the printed book because it threatened the role of calligraphy as the royal road to knowledge and preferment. It is then also, after the fall of the Ming dynasty, that Chinese culture became sterile and stopped growing and changing.

The computer is almost certain to bring about as great a change in school and learning as the printed book did, 300 and 400 years ago. The school of tomorrow is going to be technology-intensive whereas, traditionally, it has only been labor-intensive.

Needs of continuing education

Another change that is predictable, though entirely different, is that a new focus for school and learning is emerging: the continuing education of already-educated adults. Precisely because knowledge is becoming the central resource of a modern economy, continuous learning is essential. For knowledge, by its very definition, makes itself obsolete every few years, and then knowledge workers have to go back to school. They may be store managers and retail buyers, like the ones who attend your marketing university, or physicians, or engineers, but every few years they have to refresh and renew their knowledge. Otherwise they risk becoming obsolescent. This will have tremendous impact on the university and on schools. It will force us to accept the fact that, in the knowledge society, learning is life-long and does not end with graduation. In fact, that is when it begins. It will also have tremendous impact on employing institutions

In effect, these are still changes *within* the system, rather than changes *of* the system.

What is an educated person?

Your question: 'What is an educated person?' goes directly to the meaning of learning, the meaning of education the essence of the system.

I am afraid, however, that I cannot answer that question. It is going to be our challenge for the next one hundred years. In one way, I very much hope that we will be able to maintain the link with tradition and with the past, which is implicit in the traditional definition of an educated person. The Japanese definition was developed by the Bunjin of the mid-Edo period, and the Western definition was developed by the great educators of Europe's seventeenth century. These definitions still largely underlie the education that you and I received. I do not believe that this, by itself, is enough, for these definitions assume that learning is finite. They assume that an educated person is somebody who has learned while young, and stopped learning when going to work. We will now, I think, have to build into our definition what one of the great men of the Meiji period tried to establish. Yukichi Fukuzawa, truly one of the most important figures of the nineteenth century, strongly believed and preached that an educated person is one who is able and eager to continue learning. This will be particularly important as more and more young people are likely to start as specialists or, at least, will make their early careers as specialists.

Young people not knowing how to connect their knowledge

A specialist is a knowledgeable person, but he is not automatically an educated person. An educated person is capable of relating an area of special knowledge to the universe of knowledge and of human experience. This, if I may say so, is what today's younger people are not able to do. As you know, I teach mostly successful and fairly advanced executives, from business, from government, from non-profit institutions of all kinds – typically men and women in their early or mid forties – who have been successful enough to hold important executive positions, usually in large organizations. They know a great deal, but they do not know that they know it. They cannot, for instance, relate something they know about economics to their own work. They cannot relate what they know about their own work to any other field of knowledge. They do not know how to connect. This is just as true of my Japanese students as it is of my American or European students. These executives are usually brilliant people. They are sent to our Executive Management Program by their employers because they are highly promising executives. They have an outstanding educational record as a rule, and ten or fifteen years of successful, practical experience behind them, but they find it difficult to relate their experience to what their colleagues in the classroom tell them about their experiences. They find it difficult to relate what they have learned, let us say, about psychology, to their own work in managing people.

Knowledge and human development

Such people know a great many things, but they are not educated in the sense that they can reflect this knowledge on their own work or development, their own personality. This, I submit, is the great challenge ahead of us, for the next generation of educational leaders. Without it, we will have a great deal of specialized competence, but little else. The challenge ahead of us is to make knowledge again a means to human development. The challenge is to go beyond knowledge as tools and to recover education as the road to wisdom. I try to do this in my classroom and with my students. It is the one reason why I still teach at my age. Even if I am successful – and I have great doubts – I would not know how to teach this to others, let alone how to convert this into a system, a curriculum, an organized educational effort. This, in a way, is what being an educated person always meant. This is what Liberal Arts always meant. It is, in effect, what education, as distinct from knowledge competence, always meant and will, again have to mean.

December 20, 1994

Now I have hope for young people who can innovate
Isao Nakauchi

Pessimism about Japanese creativity

I am not in a position to discuss creativity in fine arts, but personally I find neither youth nor responsible people exhibit individuality in Japan.

In the past, most Japanese were members of a rural community, spending their entire lives in a simple, frugal way. Members of such a race still find it extremely difficult to act as unique individuals. Here one could suggest that in the past those in power fostered such national traits. Even in today's society, this emphasis or liking for uniformity continues in a different form, transformed by corporations, parents and children themselves. In general the result is the 'examination hell' and pedagogical methods that push students toward the goal of entering a highly-regarded company and being promoted within it later.

I am not optimistic either whether the people of Japan will come to realize the stupidity of this system. It is hard to believe that the majority will realize that it is possible to tap into the creativity and originality that lie dormant in Japanese society, to achieve something unique and reap the benefits.

Lack of a sense of self-responsibility

Unless corporations and society in general move a step toward this goal, nothing will change, regardless of the time we wait. I am personally taking steps in the direction toward creative change, but the progress is slow. Even if one makes small advances, one continually runs up against the question of how to deal with those who have already been brought up as part of the current system.

As you mentioned, at present the more successful a person has become, the harder it is to bring about reform. In all seriousness each of us has to ask: what qualities should a truly educated person have?

We have to create more opportunities for continuous learning. It seems, though, that even if corporations promote this approach, the average Japanese person lacks a sense of self-responsibility, of being responsible for his or her own education. Rather than waiting for society to solve problems, each must find his own way to a better society.

A truly educated person

To my question about defining 'educated person', you responded that it is so difficult it might take another 100 years to answer. In this regard, you once said in your *Post-Capitalist Society* that 'the educated person needs to be able to bring his or her knowledge to bear on the present, not to mention molding the future'. Here I would like to interpret this remark that a person who is truly educated is one who can bring about innovations to change the present, and which prompt changes in society. In other words, my understanding of the intent behind your words is that a good example of an educated person is a corporate executive who can push through innovations by his own efforts.

If my interpretation is correct, your words imply that executives everywhere (not only in Japan) have been entrusted with a significant task. Your letter indicates that one great challenge for truly educated people is to take what they know, to take the professional knowledge and intellectual skills they have acquired, and to use them in their own work and to form their own character – this is how they can contribute to the development of mankind.

Responsibility of executives

This is, I believe, a challenge facing all executives. They should know how to use their knowledge and skills in this way. By their own initiative, they could probably achieve positive results and exert a positive influence on today's society. It is hardly an exaggeration to say that those executives who are unable to do this, or who do not even try, are not qualified for their positions. I think that the root cause of the malaise, the lack of confidence that is now spreading throughout Japan, is to be found here.

You have given executives everywhere a tremendous challenge, a challenge that is also a difficult test. Let us hope that executives throughout the world, and from my point of view those forming the middle-level managerial staff in large Japanese organizations, will learn from the example set by people like you, or people like Yukichi Fukuzawa and other eminent leaders of the Meiji period. Hopefully, executives will realize the importance of continual learning, and will take up the great challenge that is being presented, and come out on top.

Expectation of future generations

Again I might be too optimistic here. Bringing about such changes may not be so simple. We might have to wait for the group of people now in early adulthood to mature. These are the people who are increasingly applying to join Japan Overseas Cooperation Volunteers, and are lining up for Green Cards to work in the United States. I sincerely hope that at least these young people will in time find ways to change the way of thinking in Japanese society. In a sense, I have hope for youth. And anybody can apply to join Daiei.

January 9, 1995

What changes will information technology bring to society, the economy and private enterprises?
Isao Nakauchi

The effects of information technology

The multimedia computing theme is played repeatedly throughout Japan by both public and private sectors, and by politicians. Closer analysis reveals, however, that those who repeat the theme seem more concerned with details such as telephone poles, wires and computer terminals. It appears that the word 'multimedia' has been transformed to mean the development of hardware infrastructure. This undue emphasis on hardware in the multimedia debate can be attributed to a general lack of imagination over the changes that information technology will bring to society, economy, private enterprises and individual executives.

I would like to seek your thoughts on the effects that information technology will have.

December 7, 1994

Convenience stores present an example of the information-based organization of tomorrow
Peter Drucker

The effects of information technology

I have worked hard on this question over the last five or six years. I have recently assembled my conclusions, based mostly on practical consulting work, in a major article which will appear in the January-February 1995 issue of the *Harvard Business Review* under the title 'The Information Executives Truly Need'. Let me summarize, briefly, what I tried to say in this long article.

Information needed by executives

Technological advances are forcing a reappraisal by everyone in business of what is meant by 'information'. The technology itself is only a tool, but, like every new tool, it forces us to change what we do, and not only how we do it. The main changes, however, are not changes in technology, but in our definition of information. As a result, the oldest information system businesses have, the accounting system – in the West going back 500, and possibly 700 years – will in the next twenty years be changed out of all recognition. It will be changed through the adoption of activity-based accounting which, for the first time, will enable us to have genuine control of costs, not only in manufacturing but in services as well. It will force us to do what so many Japanese companies already are doing, which is to cost the entire economic process rather than only the events that occur within the legal entity of a given enterprise – to cost the entire process from supplier, through manufacturer, to distributor and retailer, to the ultimate customer. Activity-based accounting will enable us to measure the yield from the wealth-producing activities of an enterprise, whether this is productivity or quality or innovation. It also enables measurement of the yield from the critical decisions within a business enterprise, the allocation of the two scarce resources of people and of capital. Finally, it will force us to develop information about the world outside the enterprise, where the results are. Within an enterprise there are only costs; only the customer creates results.

All this is still very much at an early stage of development, but it is already possible to describe the information system executives need and are likely to have ten or fifteen years hence. This may well become the most exciting area of management in the next decade. It is certainly the one in which there will be the greatest changes.

The superfluous *kacho*

Information technology will not only change the information we have and use. Information increasingly forms the skeleton around which we organize enterprises. Traditionally, our enterprises were organized around command and control, the only thing that was available 125 years ago when the modern business was first invented. Increasingly, we are shifting to enterprises that are organized around information. The most immediate effect of this is that we are stripping out levels of management. Even the large business enterprise of the future will have only three or, at most, four levels of management. The process of moving to that pattern has already begun, in Japan as well as in the United States, and in Europe.

The impact will, however, be greatest in Japan because it is the one country where advancement is universally seen as advancement into and through management positions. There will be very few of these positions twenty years hence. In fact there will be no *kacho* or section chief to be found. We will instead demand full information-responsibility from every individual in the organization. What, then, will that mean for traditional expectations? How will we motivate people? How will we reward people? Especially, how will we train tomorrow's senior executives, when there will be so few management levels in between?

Autonomous organizational units

These questions are beginning to be tackled. We know that one way to answer them will be to create, within the enterprise, many more autonomous units. In that respect, you and your franchised stores are very much an example of the future organization. Within the smallest convenience store, there is a sphere of managerial responsibility. The individual, small store may be completely designed by Daiei – its policies and practices worked out by Daiei, its inventory controlled by Daiei, its prices set by Daiei, and so on. The individual store owner and his wife still have a meaningful sphere of managerial responsibility, and still are being trained to run a business. We need many more units like this to prepare the executives of tomorrow in the information-based organization.

Radical change in the organization

The next question is a question about organizations in general rather than about business enterprise alone. To what extent will innovation render obsolete the traditional architecture of an organization in which employees work together in one location? Within the last few years in the US and in Europe, we have seen an enormous movement away from the traditional organization which employs the people who work for it. Instead, we have seen a shift to the use of temporary workers. I understand that this is also going on in Japan. We also see, increasingly, what is called 'outsourcing', that is, contracting out supporting activities to independent organizations. IBM, for instance, no longer itself does the data processing for its own branches, which has been transferred to a data processing company which does nothing else. Even in Japan, more and more hospitals outsource their maintenance, their supporting activities, the management of their buildings, and so on, to independent companies.

Decentralization of work

The real question is: to what extent will people continue to work in central headquarters? The largest American life insurance company, Metropolitan Life in New York, every day flies claims for insurance payments by the heirs of deceased policy-holders, to Ireland. It is a six-hour flight. The plane leaves New York at seven in the evening and arrives at six the next morning, given the time difference. At eight, the claims are already being worked on by Irish staff. Ireland has the highest unemployment rate in Europe and an excellent school system, so that a good supply of well-schooled people are available to process insurance claims. By five p.m. Irish time – noon in New York – these claims have been processed, the checks have been written and enveloped with the address of the American payee. By six p.m. they are back on the plane. Six hours later they are back in New York where it is six in the afternoon, and an hour later they are on overnight planes to their destinations. The heirs of the deceased policy-holders receive their checks next morning. The same approach is being used with check clearing for the banks, with draftsman work for architect practices, and with interpretation of electrocardiograms for isolated hospitals.

Working at home and the satellite office

A great achievement of the nineteenth century was to enable people to become mobile. In Japan, for example, there were large pilgrimages in earlier times, in which a whole village went to a great shrine, but this was a once-in-a-lifetime event. The nineteenth century saw the introduction of mass travel by steamship, railroad, streetcar, bicycle, automobile and, finally, airplane.

The twentieth century has seen the ready movement of ideas and information. People occupy a lot of space and are expensive to move, and the capacity of most big cities to move them is increasingly strained beyond breaking point, as one visit to Tokyo's Shinjuku station at eight in the morning will demonstrate. In fact there is only one major city in the world today in which public transportation still functions. It is Chicago. Tokyo and Osaka, New York, Los Angeles, London, Paris have all become nightmares. This is no longer necessary. Most of the people who move and commute every day into the centers of the big cities need not be there. For the clerical work that they do – the handling of information – they do not need to meet anybody. How many of those people will in the future work at home is hotly debated. In the United States, about four per cent of the work-force in big organizations now works at home, with another twenty per cent in small office clusters outside the big city. They have telephones, fax machines, closed-circuit television (increasingly interactive television) and so there is no need for them to spend hours commuting into the big city in the morning, and hours going home.

In the West, it is predictable that twenty-five years hence the great majority of employees in our business and government organizations will not commute to work. The work will commute to them. I am not so sure that this is going to happen as fast in Japan. Seeing each other, working in contact with one another, working in the place with the right address, are far more important in Japan than they are in the West. But I am convinced that we all are moving in the same direction. In fact, in one area, Japan has already gone further than the West – in your creation of the science city of Tsukuba.

The cohesion of tomorrow's organization

What this will mean for future organizations is very hard to predict. How do we maintain the cohesion of people who work for the same firm but never see each other? Again, you at Daiei have probably gone further in showing us how to do this than the large manufacturing companies. For your thousands of stores work as one organization even though the people who work in them do not see each other physically and have very little contact with each other. You already bring the work to them. We will have to learn from you how to maintain the cohesion of the large organization even though its employees are no longer in physical contact, except on very rare occasions such as an anniversary or a social event.

An unpredictable future for office city

What will this do to society? What does the future hold for city centers, that is, for the office city?

The real-estate boom which created today's big cities began in Japan with the establishment of Edo, that is, three hundred and fifty years ago. It started in the West a little later, with the great fire of London in the latter half of the seventeenth century. It has continued, almost unabated, even through periods of depression. Is it over? Will the city of tomorrow still be a place where people work? Or will it be a governmental, ceremonial, educational, artistic center, only?

The city as we know it first arose as a government unit. Kamakura, Kyoto, and Edo were basically centers of government, and so were the cities of medieval Europe. The nineteenth century city, based on our ability to move people, became a manufacturing city. The city after World War II has become an office city. Pre-War, if a movie showed skyscrapers, you knew that you were looking at either New York or Chicago. I went recently to Shizuoka, which I first knew thirty-seven years ago as a small and sleepy industrial city. It is now a city of skyscrapers. So are many other cities, even small ones, in the developed and developing worlds. All these skyscrapers are office buildings. Can they survive, or are they rapidly becoming museum-pieces and relics of the world before the Information Revolution?

This, I submit, is one of the most critical questions to ask, and I do not know the answer.

Impact of information on one's way of life

I am reasonably sure that information technology will radically and profoundly change the school, the business organization, and the city. As you point out, 'hard' infrastructure is not the most important thing in the world to worry about. There is an enormous amount of technical change going on in computer technology, in software technology, and so on. But the really important questions are the impact on our vision of the world, on the way we work and on the way we live. Information has created a global consciousness. Everybody today gets the same information, and that much of it distorts reality is perhaps not too relevant. It still conveys the same data to everybody. What is equally important, it interprets the data the same way, for example by selecting what is being shown on the evening television newscast. Information is changing the meaning of learning and teaching profoundly. It is changing organizational structure and with it, the careers and expectations of people. It may change the way we live. With modern information delivery there is no rural isolation anymore. Everybody lives in the same information universe, and it is essentially an urban universe.

What information technology adds to the old ways

One thing, however, can be said with reasonable probability: the new will not drive out the old. Forty years ago, some very intelligent friends of mine predicted that television would make the book obsolete. Everybody, everywhere now has television – when considering television, there are no 'underdeveloped' countries. Yet the number of books published and bought has increased greatly in all developed countries, in Japan as much as the United States, Great Britain, or Germany. People who never before bought a book, let alone read one, now buy a book after they have seen on television the movie made from it.

Something very similar happened when the printed book was introduced. One of the great minds of the European Renaissance, the great Erasmus – he lived in the early years of the sixteenth century – predicted that the printed book would mean the end of letter-writing. The opposite happened. The great age of letter-writing in Western civilization began around 1600, that is, when reading books became universal. It reached its peak when everybody had become literate because of the printed book, that is, at the end of the nineteenth century.

In other words, the new does not replace the old. It adds to it. I think one can expect the same to happen with information, although the center of gravity shifts. My grandchildren, most of them now in their mid-twenties and graduated from college, take modern information for granted. It has become their tool. What they want to do with it, however, are very traditional things. One of them, for instance, is a musician. Another is about to become an architect. How they do their work, however, is already different. Whether, as you fear, information will diminish creativity and imagination, I very much doubt. But it will take different forms, and they are already visible.

December 20, 1994

Developments in IT will transform every worker into an executive
Isao Nakauchi

The impact of information technology

Your letter made clear to me how the development of information technologies could impact an economy and society in ways that were beyond reach of my imagination.

As information technology develops, it makes outsourcing possible, and enables each organization to become compact. As this process continues, the conventional hierarchical organization quickly loses its effectiveness. Many well-established corporations have no choice but to make maximum use of the blessings that information technologies have to offer, reforming their organizations so that they are based on principles set down for the information age. If they do not, they lose their competitiveness.

How, then, can we characterize an organization that can take advantage of information revolution? The example of the convenience store system points us to the realization that such a business is extremely compact and so devolves managerial responsibility to everyone within the organization. I believe that this point is very important. If managerial responsibility is devolved to all, they are also given responsibility to innovate, to exert an influence on present circumstances. This also means that they must use knowledge and skills at their own initiative, and need to apply their talents to the work. Development of information technology will create many autonomous departments within each corporation and will transform each person in every department into an executive in his or her own right. Expressed differently, the development of information technology can create 'executives of tomorrow' who will have an impact on the ways of the society. There is no doubt at all that this will be a welcome improvement.

Creation of the 'executives of tomorrow'

It must be said, though, that discussion of this topic in Japan is unfortunately very rare. Even when comment is made, all that is usually said is that the development of information technology will transform current hierarchical organizations into flat networks. No effort is made to explain this or expand upon it. The media just blabs on about how, for example, the information age will steal jobs from middle management, and how employees who do not know how to use a personal computer will be of no use to a company.

As information technology develops, as you pointed out, there will be no need for the traditional Japanese manager, nor for employees lacking knowledge and training concerning personal computers. There may be additional jobs created by the introduction of personal computers. Is there not an absolute need, by using information technology, to reorganize our enterprises into independent divisions standing on the foundation of information, and, through continuous training, a member of such a division must become an 'executives of tomorrow'?

I believe your comments are alarms to a Japan that is too hardware-oriented. As an executive, it is my earnest hope that many Japanese people will read your response and become fully aware of the responsibilities that one must bear and of the tasks that lie ahead of them.

January 9, 1995

4

The challenges for entrepreneurship and innovation

The entrepreneur's role in society is to bring innovation
Isao Nakauchi

Necessary conditions for innovation

The great economist Schumpeter once said that innovation arising from the original ideas of entrepreneurs will result in rapid economic growth. A problem in Japan today is that the number of entrepreneurs appears to be declining. Top positions are increasingly filled by the promotion of ordinary managers who happen to be effective administrators. This leaves me in no doubt that the future will be dim, even for businesses enjoying strong balance sheets now. Has Japan already become a country that cannot produce true entrepreneurs? Will large corporations, saddled with ossified pyramid structures, never again become the bearers of innovation? To make matters worse, even small- and medium-sized enterprises do not seem to produce leaders any more.

In this regard, I would like to pose a question, Professor Drucker. In the light of your considerable experience, could you please tell us what we need to create the basic conditions to enable Japan – a country currently in a dejected mood – to push strongly for innovations in all fields, including the financial sector?

Roles for entrepreneurs

My second question on innovation relates to what will probably become a very important factor when predicting the future of post-capitalist societies.

As I recall Schumpeter's vision of society, the spirit of entrepreneurs is very important, yet innovation arising from the individual efforts of entrepreneurs eventually comes to an end, as does economic development. In an extreme case, capitalism may give way to socialism. This vision of society, considered alongside the decline in the number of Japanese entrepreneurs, appears to indicate that Schumpeter's thesis is becoming a reality. There is some speculation that, in Japan, the many government regulations are driving innovative people to start their businesses abroad.

Against this background, where could innovations come from in Japan? Will the future be drab and without vitality, and will time simply pass us by? Is the word 'innovation' on the way to being forgotten in Japan? As one who has for many years striven to reform Japan's distribution structure, believing that an entrepreneur's role in society is to bring about innovation, I find it harrowing to have to ask these questions.

I am sure that you have had many occasions to provide encouragement to Japanese businessmen. Please be kind enough to tell us again your present views on what should be the role expected of entrepreneurs today, and what will happen to innovation.

After reading these questions, you may be tempted to think that I want pampering, and that I should answer these questions myself, as a Japanese executive. In today's Japan there is a tendency to look only at the immediate present, not the future, and we have little sense of self-respect. Please consider our present status in providing suggestions.

December 7, 1994

I am confident that a third 'economic miracle' will happen in Japan
Peter Drucker

YOU ARE ABSOLUTELY RIGHT. In the next five or ten years, every developed country and every major business within it, will have to learn to innovate. Also, every country will have to learn to how to encourage and develop entrepreneurs. This is by no means limited to Japan, but the need may be greatest in Japan, and most difficult to satisfy.

The effect of 'creative imitation'

Perhaps I had best begin by saying that Japan can probably continue to do very well on its present course, in which entrepreneurship mostly consists in doing better – often much better – what other developed countries are already doing well. The great successes of Japan, which made Japan a world leader and an economic power of the first rank, were largely in industries which were developed well before World War II, and mostly in the 1920s: automobiles, consumer electronics, steel, ship building, and so on. There are probably going to be substantial markets for these high-engineering products of the past, at least for another fifteen or twenty years. They are exactly the products which rapidly developing countries need the most and value the most.

If mainland Asia continues to grow and to develop, it will, for the foreseeable future, be a major market for products of this kind. The one traditional area in which, I believe, Japan will have to change dramatically is probably finance. In many ways, finance is the number one growth area of the next ten years. Demographics alone will make sure of that, as older people will become the dominant population in developed country after developed country. Even here, what the Japanese financial industry has to achieve is to be a little better in markets where the financial industries of the West, led by the United States, are already present. In finance, too, I foresee a great opportunity to become a leader by improving on what is already being done, rather than by genuine innovation.

But that is not the future. It is catching up with the past. The future clearly demands a shift to very different industries and different services. With Japan now a world leader, the country cannot hope to maintain its leadership position by what I have been calling 'creative imitation.'

Decline of entrepreneurship

Let me emphasize that, in this respect, Japan is not alone. This challenge faces every one of the developed countries, but the challenge may be most acute in Japan. Creative imitation has been extraordinarily successful in your country, and it is always very difficult to argue with success.

Amongst the developed countries, Japan has the most successful entrepreneurial history. There is no country that can equal the entrepreneurial performance of Japan after the Pacific War. As you point out, in Japan – but by no means in Japan alone – there are signs of diminishing entrepreneurial vigor just when we need it the most.

We actually know what is needed. There is, in fact, no excuse for any country, for any economy, for any industry, for any company, not to be innovative.

Two parallel needs concerning entrepreneurship

We know, first, that we face two parallel but separate challenges. We need entrepreneurs who can start new businesses outside established companies. We need, in other words, people like you were thirty or forty years ago, or people like the other major architect of Japanese retail in the last forty years, my old friend, Ito Masatoshi. We need people like Honda, like Morita Akio of Sony, and many others – the people who created today's Japanese economy and society, and did it by building businesses outside the existing system.

We also need to build into the existing business a capacity to innovate. If the existing business does not learn to become entrepreneurial and innovative, we face far too much social dislocation.

How to organize for entrepreneurship and innovation

Secondly, we know how to organize for entrepreneurship and innovation. We have the discipline for it, although forty years ago, when you started, it did not exist. We know that innovation begins with looking at the changes that have already happened in economy, in society and in technology, in order to find the opportunities for successful innovation. As you know, I wrote a book on this, some ten years ago. The title is *Innovation and Entrepreneurship*, so I shall not bore you or our readers by repeating what this book reported as a result of my forty years of work in this area. It is not difficult, in fact, to become innovative.

Young people are required

The next issue is something else again, at least for Japan. Innovation and entrepreneurship require young people. Unless you start to innovate in your twenties or, at the latest, in your early thirties, you will never do it. You yourself, if I may say so, were barely thirty when you started to build what is now Daiei. Morita was twenty seven or twenty eight when he began to build what is now Sony. Honda was not much older. Matsushita was even younger. And the men of the Meiji period were all in their late twenties when they began. Shibusawa Eiichi (whom I consider the real father of modern Japan), founded the first modern Japanese bank when he was thirty. Fukuzawa Yukichi published his first important book when he was twenty six, and founded Keio University when he was thirty seven. Iwasaki Yataro established what is now known as Mitsubishi when he was twenty six. The same is true in every country. Innovators and entrepreneurs have to start early.

This may be the greatest challenge for Japan. It requires changes in the financial system so that young entrepreneurs can have access to capital. To the best of my knowledge, there is no way of obtaining venture capital in Japan, today. But, above all, it requires tremendous changes in the way big companies are organized, especially drastic changes in the way existing companies manage their younger people. That it can be done is demonstrated by the example of two American companies that are among the world's largest businesses but which have managed to remain innovative. One is 3M, the world's leader in half a dozen different industries; the other one is Johnson & Johnson, the world's leader in a wide variety of health-care products. In both you cannot gain admission to senior management unless you proposed a new product before you were thirty, and then built a successful business on it.

How do you build this approach into the existing successful, large company? I am not talking of Japanese companies alone. We have the same problem in the United States and in Europe.

Innovators do not work in a team

In Japan the problem may be most difficult and most acute. One reason is that innovators are not team-players. Innovation cannot be done by committee. As you exemplify, it is highly individual and very lonely. Successful innovators build teams, but they do not work in a team. They work alone and by themselves. This is not what existing, large companies want and tolerate, let alone encourage. Yet, it is what they will have to learn to do. It requires changes in rewards. It requires that young people, in the first ten years of work within a company, are challenged to step out of line and make radical suggestions for change – and that the company then encourages them and sets them up to perform what they have promised. It requires that society values and respects the individual entrepreneur who starts a business on his own, rather than give all approval to the organization man.

Role of pioneers

You may say that these are radical changes, and changes which are all but impossible for Japanese companies, and Japanese society. In fact, when I discuss these things with my friends, I am being told that I am talking of a cultural revolution. My American or German friends are very often just as skeptical as my Japanese friends. But what happened in Japan in the Meiji era, and what happened forty years ago in the 1950s, represent even more radical cultural revolutions. In fact, we do not need to have every company change the way it manages to bring about such a cultural revolution. In the 1950s, when I first visited Japan, the great majority of businesses were still managed the way Japanese businesses had been managed fifty years earlier. It took only two or three companies to pioneer a radically new corporate culture – one focused on continuing quality, on continuing improvement, on becoming multinational. At first, these few companies had a very difficult time. The financial community did not understand what they were doing. MITI, and other government agencies, were opposed to them. They found it difficult at first to attract first-rate people. Only five years or so later, their success had become apparent, and then it took only another five years before what had been the rare exceptions became the rule. It takes only a few successful pioneers to show the way.

The years of tremendous change

As you point out, there is urgent need – and not in Japan alone – for developed economies and for all existing businesses within them, to become innovative. The next ten years will be years of tremendous change. They will be years in which the centres of gravity in every developed economy will shift from the developed industries of today, to new industries. They are years in which traditional services, such as retailing, will be delivered in radically new ways. They are years that demand another economic miracle akin to what happened in Japan forty years ago.

This is the challenge which your questions raise. I am confident that it will be met in Japan. The young Japanese I know are ready for it, but it will require a tremendous new effort, and tremendous new dedication.

I hope that this answers your important questions – and I hope that Japanese business listens to your questions and responds to them.

December 20, 1994

'Creation of customers' will be an eternal challenge
Isao Nakauchi

The 'creative imitation' of Japanese companies

In response to my question, you pointed out that, while Japan is not alone in needing to learn innovative ways to foster entrepreneurs, the issue is more pronounced and more difficult to carry out in Japan than elsewhere. The reason you gave was that large corporations in Japan have been excellent at 'creative imitation' of Europe and America, and poor at developing new industries or services from scratch.

Your words have given me a pause for thought. My own experience at Daiei – introducing the chain store and franchising approaches among other things – was, in retrospect, nothing more than creative imitation of methods developed in the United States.

The same judgment can be applied not only to Daiei, but to most businesses that enjoyed rapid growth after World War II. If this is so, then we must conclude that the Japanese economy is incapable of leading the world in the future.

New materials

In response to my letter on information technology, you said that the new should not replace the old but complement it. This surely represents the 'new combination' espoused by Schumpeter, the essence of innovation that Japanese business must again learn to appreciate.

Until now, Japanese businesses have practiced and succeeded in creative imitation by monitoring what is happening in the United States. Without a doubt, we still have much to learn from the United States where innovation can be found in many areas. If we are to learn, we need to make the transition from studying the outcome of innovation to studying ways to produce it. We have no time to be disheartened.

In your essay 'Reflections of a Social Ecologist' in *The Ecological Vision*, you stress the importance of identifying and analyzing the future that has already happened, citing social and economic transitions in Japan during the early 1960s as an example. Similarly, your latest letter points out that the many outstanding successes of business leaders since the Meiji Restoration should be viewed by today's Japanese executives in the context of the 'future which has already happened,' and then to add something new to this. At this point, I would like to reflect on my own experience in examining the 'future which has already happened' in Japanese history.

After the experience in the jungle

From June 1945 until the end of the war on 15 August, I was wandering around the depths of the jungle in the Philippines, a wounded soldier of the defeated Japanese army. There was no food, I had to eat anything I could find to stay alive somehow, even the leather from my boots. This was certainly no time to ponder lofty ideology or ideals. Only the thought of how I wanted to fill my stomach with *sukiyaki* kept me going until I made it home.

Returning to my homeland, learning for the first time of the sad reality of war, and reflecting on the tragedy of so many lost comrades, I asked myself how the normally-sensible Japanese could have started on such a senseless venture.

I concluded that two things were necessary in order to prevent Japan from committing such a senseless act in the future. First, we would need to maintain friendly relations with other countries. Secondly, it would be necessary to modernize the distribution structure and build a national network allowing all Japanese citizens to purchase the goods they want at the desired price, time and location, just as veins pump nutrients around the human body. This brought me to the concept of American supermarkets.

The message of John F. Kennedy

I was very busy with the daily tasks of business after opening the first Daiei store in 1957. However, my visit to the United States in 1962 to represent Japan at the 25th Annual Supermarket Institute Convention marked a major turning point. Each word of greeting offered by President Kennedy opened new vistas to my eyes.

The President celebrated the supermarket, noting that supermarkets supported affluent consumer lifestyles of the United States, and stressed that the society of convenience that supermarkets could bring was exactly the type of society that all Americans wanted.

Deeply impressed by his words, I visited supermarkets at all available opportunities. Again, I was impressed by what I could verify with my own eyes. American supermarkets really were fully consumer-oriented, geared toward achieving the four rights of consumers espoused by President Kennedy in March 1962, and furthermore providing a service to local communities.

Wisdom learned from America

This experience in the United States, coupled with my beliefs concerning the founding of Daiei, convinced me that modernization of the distribution structure in order to provide a service to consumers and society would create stability in the lives of the people, maintain a healthy society, and also create a peaceful society. Some might criticize this kind of statement as the extravagance of a company founder, but I think it was definitely this conviction, gained in the early 1960s, which served as the driving force behind the growth of Daiei to where it stands today.

I believe that the post-War growth of many Japanese companies can be attributed to a common desire to lift the country quickly out of its sorry state and to improve the quality of life for the people, with the conviction gained in the United States that their efforts would not be in vain. For many companies, this conviction provided the strength to achieve phenomenal growth, in turn enabling the rapid economic growth of the nation.

So what did Japanese business learn from the United States? Certainly, we learned specific business techniques such as product development, marketing, and financial management. But I believe that the greatest influence on Japanese business, the most important lesson of all, was the deeply-ingrained spirit of service to consumers and society in American business, as illustrated by supermarkets. Of all the things we learned from the United States, this surely has the greatest significance because Japanese companies did more than just copy American management techniques. They learned the universal spirit of service, or what you describe as wisdom. And it was this wisdom that supported rapid economic growth in Japan.

Drucker's suggestions

It was then, struck by the suggestion for 'customer creation' in your excellent work *The Practice of Management*, that I understood the significance of business. Although taking a risk with money was seen in Japan at that time as a greedy act, your proposition – that the purpose of business is to create customers – gave me the courage to confront the prevailing social mood.

I hope to build our business in China, slowly if necessary but surely, drawing upon my experiences with the founding of Daiei. China today is akin to Japan in about 1960, in that society tends to view the act of risking money to start a business as 'money-worshipping' and greedy. but this does not mean that risking money is always bad. People will continue to risk their money to achieve comfort and well-being, and it is this motive that provides the driving force behind economic vitality. As an executive who enjoys the benefits of the world economy, I believe that one of my responsibilities is to assist the people of China in making the transition from the stage where they are busy just trying to obtain food and clothing, to the stage of affluence and well-being.

Service to consumers and society

Professor Drucker, through your words I recalled the wisdom I gained during my visit to the United States over 30 years ago. I feel the enthusiasm I felt then as I realize the functions and duties I must fulfill, both within and outside the company. This is both an enormous responsibility and a highly appealing challenge.

Like you, I am determined to apply myself to the major challenge of eternal learning, to a greater degree than before. Through this, I hope to tell not just Daiei but all of Japan, and even the world, about my experience – how peace can be brought through modernization of distribution in line with the spirit of service to consumers and society.

Many executives in Japan have heard your words. It is now up to them either to follow or ignore your advice. However, Japanese executives are not fools, so they will surely heed you – that the wisdom built up over time can be linked to one's own work. If not – if they are not magnanimous enough to take on this duty – then talk of corporate activity and economic and social resurgence in Japan, let alone our international contribution, becomes meaningless. It may well be that, as you say, the understanding by executives of their responsibilities will hold the key to the revitalization of Japan.

January 9, 1995

5

Appendix to Part I

Correspondence concerning the Great Hanshin-
Awaji Earthquake of January 17, 1995

January 17, 1995

Dear Mr Nakauchi

We just heard the news of the terrible earthquake in the Osaka-
Kobe area, and are very much concerned about the safety of
all our Japanese friends. Please let me know how you and
your family are doing – and did any of your stores suffer
great damage? I hope everybody and everything is safe.

With best regards

Peter Drucker

January 17, 1995

Dear Professor Drucker

Thank you very much for your fax expressing your concern
over the earthquake in the Osaka-Kobe area.

You may rest assured that we are safe, but our stores in the
Kobe area suffered severe damage. We are trying our utmost
to resume regular operations in the earliest future.

Thank you once again for your concern.

Sincerely yours,

Isao Nakauchi

January 30, 1995

Dear Mr Nakauchi

I just got terrible news about the loss of life among Daiei employees and families in the Kobe earthquake. Please accept my most sincere condolences. I know that Daiei has also suffered tremendous losses in its stores in the Kobe area, and I grieve for those too. But property losses will soon be made good and forgotten. Losing members of the Daiei team, associates and employees, one never forgets. So I am sending you my deepest sympathy and my warmest wishes to you and all your associates at Daiei on this terrible tragedy. Next autumn, when I plan to be back in Japan, I hope to be able to express my sympathy and my condolences to you in person.

In the meantime my warmest regards and best wishes

Peter Drucker

February 1, 1995

Dear Professor Drucker

Thank you very much for your letter expressing your concern over the earthquake in the Kobe area and our employees and families.

The loss of life among Daiei Group staff was not insignificant, and our stores in the area have also been severely damaged. However, at the moment we are putting our maximum efforts into restoring our regular operations in order to provide our customers with stable supply of daily necessities.

Thank you once again for your concern and hope to see you in autumn.

Sincerely yours,

Isao Nakauchi

February 25, 1995

Dear Professor Drucker

First I would like you to accept my apologies for being late in responding to your letter and would like to express my gratitude to you.

A thoughtful letter that fateful morning

Early in the morning of January 17, after the Great Hanshin Earthquake, I received a fax from you expressing your concern. On the morning of 30 January, I received another fax expressing your condolences for the many employees and family members of the Daiei Group who were killed in the disaster. When I read these two letters my heart was deeply moved by your kindness and thoughtfulness, which reached out to me from across the wide distance that separates Japan and the United States. In your letter, you stated, 'Property losses will be made good and forgotten. Losing members of the Daiei team, associates and employees one never forgets.' I do indeed feel deep sadness at the fact that some of my colleagues and members of their families have died in this disaster. More than 5,000 people have died in the areas affected by the disaster, including 118 Daiei employees and family members (as of February 10).

Establishing an Emergency Management Center

The earthquake struck at 5:46 on the morning of January 17. I first heard about it at 5:55 on the television news at my home in Tokyo. Considering the scale of the disaster, I instructed staff to set up a control center to handle store damage reports received from the quake zone while in my car on the way to work. The Daiei Emergency Management Center was thus established at 7:00 and immediately set to work. A similar Center was set up in Kobe itself, and Daiei stores in the area (most of which were closed for holidays taken instead of the New Year break) were ordered to reopen to provide the everyday necessities to those affected by the disaster. Preparations were made to transport some 360 relief workers from Tokyo and Kyushu, together with supplies to the Kobe Emergency Management Center. By the time they left, at 10:00, new damage reports pouring in described a scale of devastation previously unimaginable.

I resolved that our Daiei stores and Lawson convenience store outlets should remain open, operating from car parks if stores proved unusable, or at the very least provided with lighting where trading itself proved unfeasible. I could still remember the feeling of unease associated with being in a war-devastated area devoid of human activity, and the subsequent relief and hope as the lights gradually returned to the streets. Simultaneously, incoming earthquake reports indicated an escalating level of damage.

Making full efforts toward recovery

Daiei had 49 outlets in the areas affected by the disaster, but as a result of the earthquake, 11 of those are unable to conduct business. Furthermore, it is expected that the total loss from destruction of store buildings and loss to inventory will reach 50 billion yen. As a result, for the first time since its founding, Daiei is facing a crisis in which it expects to report a loss at the end of the current fiscal year.

However, this is not a time for us to immerse ourselves in the tragedy. Daiei is determined to devote its full efforts to recovering from this disaster, in part as a tribute to the colleagues whom we have lost, and to support the lives of the people in the areas affected by the disaster. Kobe is the birthplace of Daiei, where it began as a chain store, and I, too, am from Kobe. As someone directly affected by this disaster, I devote my fullest efforts to overcoming this greatest disaster since World War II, together with all of the people who are rising toward recovery.

At the same time, I feel pride in the fact that in order to fulfill its responsibility to the people of the disaster areas as a supplier, my colleagues, even while worrying about their own damaged homes and displaced families, devoted themselves to retail operations. I believe that we contributed to making the city a brighter and better place.

Importance of distribution in a disaster area

This earthquake made me recognize anew the importance of distribution. Even one week after the disaster, it was not possible for significant traffic to flow along the narrowed roads of the areas affected. As a result, chaos reigned, and even when fire broke out, fire engines were unable to approach the scene.

This meant it was impossible to deliver the necessary goods as we would have liked. Meanwhile, the very needs of the residents of the disaster areas changed every day. From the first through the third days there was a great need for drinking water and ready meals that could be eaten immediately; on the fourth day, there was a need for clothing; on the fifth day, there was a need for portable gas stoves and eating plates and bowls.

To meet appropriately the needs of customers, which were changing every day, our priority was to secure a route for the transport of products. We could not wait until the traffic barriers disappeared. For that reason, Daiei established, as its top priority, the reconstruction of its logistics system all the way down to the retail outlets, and although there was confusion, on the day that the earthquake broke out, Daiei arranged for helicopters, ferries, tank rollers, trucks and other means of transportation, secured a transport route for products to be moved to the disaster area using marine transport from the nearest port, and carried some goods to the disaster areas using heliports. Furthermore, we sent an emergency dispatch of employees from all over the country to speed the recovery of the Kobe distribution center, which was the key to logistics in the disaster area. Moreover, for the retail outlets that suffered damage, we gathered personnel from Tokyo and other regions on the very day of the earthquake and had them working for recovery. At stores where operations were possible, we extended the hours for customers who had traveled long distances in search of open shops. At stores that had collapsed, we established temporary sales locations in parking lots and other available spaces and continued to provide a supply of necessities.

Through such efforts, as the days passed, the number of stores that could carry out operations increased, and we continued to supply the basic needs. Nonetheless, the damage from this unprecedented earthquake disaster far exceeded all expectations, and we cannot say that Daiei was 100% in its response. I have come to feel that parts of our response were continually delayed. For chain stores – just as with telephones, electricity, water, gas and other utility supplies – in a transition from a normal period to a state of emergency, how quickly can we implement the logistics for supplying the necessities, which serve as a lifeline for people? Can our structure for that state of emergency actually function? These are two important points in thinking about risk management for a disaster situation like this.

Confusion caused by lack of information

Another important point is information. The mass media have had a field-day in criticizing the incapacity of the national and local governments to respond to the crisis. Personally, when I went to the disaster areas, I keenly felt the slow response of the administration, and I believe that the main factor in that was the lack of information. Even in our response, especially during the initial stages, there was confusion resulting from lack of information. This was an issue stemming

91

from infrastructure aspects, in that our traditional wire-based network was pushed beyond its limits. However, I think that there were also some important points regarding processes, such as the modalities for communicating information about total capacity, and judgments and directives relevant to information processing. The overtly compartmentalized structures that exist in government bureaucracies and large corporations cannot be thought of as an effective way to process information at times like this.

Reconstruction led by the private sector

However, it is not a time for criticizing others now. The important question is the future. We cannot build a bright future through a war of words. What the Daiei Group must do now is to continue to serve the people of the disaster area, to help them recover as quickly as possible. In the recovery process, we must not allow ourselves to think 'This is something that the central or local government should do.' Rather, as private-sector corporations and individual citizens, we must cling to the concept 'We will rebuild Kobe ourselves,' and we must display vitality in a spirit of initiative, self-offering, self-discipline and self-responsibility to achieve a recovery of the disaster area. Daiei will participate fully in this.

Professor Drucker, I believe that whether the private sector can serve as the primary force in the recovery of the disaster areas is a litmus test of whether Japan can become. a truly civilized society. For that reason, as a person affected by this disaster, I intend to work for the recovery of the affected areas, with the residents of those regions.

In that process, let me again thank you for the two extremely kind letters of encouragement that you sent me. Let me tell you that these two letters will serve as an inspiration for me, and I will use them to bolster my energy to face tomorrow.

Sincerely yours,

Isao Nakauchi

Part II

Time to Reinvent

6

Reinventing the individual

Japan urgently needs to reinvigorate ordinary
people and make them more effective
Isao Nakauchi

PROFESSOR DRUCKER, I AM SURE that your books and
articles have given many executives courage. I can but hope
that they have taken your words to heart. So that I may con-
vey your messages to executives throughout Japan and the
world, I would like to ask you some questions that arise in
response to your letter, with particular reference to the issue
of revitalization.

Reinvigorating individuals in the organization

Through your writings, you have explained that a kind of
cultural revolution is necessary for Japan. In particular, you
have mentioned that there is a need to create structures that
will allow employees to create innovation, in matters such as
new product development, while they are still young. On
this point, I think that your way of thinking is completely
correct.

If we are to say that corporate culture has gone too far in
Japan, then we must create a climate where not only individual people with specialized skills but all workers participate in innovation, precisely because each of them is an 'ordinary person'. Each of them achieving results and sharing

95

in the joy of reinvigorating the organization.

It is certainly true that there are very few individuals who can effect innovation. Such individuals usually possess an abundance of independent spirit and tend to strive to display their capabilities outside firmly established organizations. As a result, most people who remain in large organizations are basically 'ordinary people'.

Corporations must continue to give ordinary staff opportunities to be involved in innovation, and give them opportunities to feel the joy of working. In other words, we can understand as an ideal proposition that, no matter what cost is involved, corporations should maintain employment. Actually, many Japanese corporations, to effect that ideal, seconded or transferred employees to subsidiaries within their group as situations became worse during the current recession. Where that did not improve operations, they cut salaries to maintain employment.

However, we cannot ignore the fact that such Japanese-style employment practices have robbed Japanese enterprises of one major tool of management. It then becomes very difficult to turn around a badly-performing corporation.

In contrast to this type of corporation, many American businesses implement wide-reaching restructuring from time to time, and successfully turn around bad performance in a dramatic manner. I could describe a common restructuring that American corporations pursue as laying off ordinary workers while hiring a smaller number of ' knowledge workers' to increase intellectual productivity, so improving total productivity. It is an indisputable fact that this method can be immediately effective.

Consideration has recently been given to personnel restructuring even in Japan, including high-volume layoffs. Primarily this is in corporations whose performance has become extremely poor. From this, we can infer that Japanese corporate behavior has already begun to change fundamentally.

I have a feeling that there is a vanishingly thin line between whether what Japanese corporations are trying to do now will lead to a true 'cultural revolution', or will just invite 'cultural destruction.'

Efforts of individuals to be effective

Finding a rule for ordinary people who cannot innovate except as a part of some kind of organizations will become an issue. As an executive, I fully understand that, in Japan, the decision-making process regarding layoffs is certainly no easy one. The manager visualizes, one by one, the faces of those who will be laid off and thinks of their respective families. The fact that the top executives of corporations· that have decided to conduct large-scale layoffs sometimes resign as a way of taking responsibility for that act clearly speaks of the difficulty of laying off workers in Japan.

What Japan urgently needs now is to reinvigorate the many ordinary people and make them more effective. However, unless the individuals concerned realize the need for change, there will not be a solution. I believe that what is important is for the individuals themselves to feel a 'brightness' about what is to come.

What kind of will does an ordinary person need to become effective? What sort of effort do they need to make? I would be very happy if you could give me your honest opinion on these points.

January 9, 1995

Knowledge people must take responsibility for their development and placement
Peter Drucker

How to cause changes

By way of introduction, permit me to say that I doubt that many of our readers will realize that the questions you are asking me would not have been asked only a few short decades ago.

Concern about the health of society is very old. It was extensively discussed in the writings attributed to Confucius. In the West, it was discussed extensively, and at about the same time, by both great Greek philosophers, Plato and Aristotle. The question was always: 'How can we restore society?' Your questions, 'How we anticipate change?', 'How can we make organizations create the future?', and 'How can we manage change?', these are new questions. They really have come to the forefront only in the last forty year or so. The question about the individual, the first of your questions, is a brand-new one, as I shall shortly explain.

'The Awareness of change' has changed

That these questions now seem obvious to us, bespeaks a profound change, in both our views of society and organizations, and in the reality in which we live. It is not only that we are so conscious of change. This is nothing very new. Though we live in a period of great and rapid changes, there have been earlier periods in the history of all civilizations in which changes were equally great and equally rapid. The common belief that technology moves much faster these days than it ever did before is largely a delusion.

No technology in recent years has diffused faster than did eyeglasses, an invention of the late thirteenth century. They spread in fifty years from Oxford in England to the Court of the Pope of the Catholic Church at Avignon in France, to the Court of the Sultan of Egypt in Cairo, and to the Court of the Chinese Emperor. Printing with moveable type, as it was discovered (or, rather, rediscovered) in Germany around 1440 had, twenty years later, spread throughout Europe, with some fifty thousand books printed before the year 1500. And nothing in this century has moved faster than three American inventions of the nineteenth century – the electric light bulb, the sewing machine, and the typewriter. Each spread worldwide within ten years of its invention.

What has changed, and changed profoundly, is our awareness of change. In the past, change was always seen as the anomalous, the exception, perhaps as something that should not be allowed to happen. Societies and groups were organized to prevent change and to maintain stability. We now realize that this does not work. Society and groups have to be organized to take advantage of change.

The first change – social mobility

For the individual, we have a totally new situation. In the past there was no point in asking how individuals could maintain their vitality, their ability to grow, their ability to learn, their ability to change. In the first place, almost no-one, as recently as a hundred years ago, had to cope with change. Most people stayed in the economic and social class into which they were born. Even in times of dramatic social change, such as the first twenty years of the Meiji era in Japan or, somewhat earlier, the first thirty years after the Napoleonic Wars in Western Europe, very few people had social mobility. There was therefore, little need to learn. The boy who was born on a farm and grew up on it, knew everything he needed to know to be a farmer for the rest of his life by the time he was fifteen. Even where skill was needed, the apprentices had learned everything they would ever need to know for the rest of their working life by the time they were eighteen or nineteen years old.

Two things have changed, and they are closely connected. One is that today we have tremendous social mobility, especially through education. This is something that never happened before. The tremendous achievement of the Meiji era was the immediate recognition that education was the way to create social mobility. Meiji Japan understood that education enabled capable young people to move out of the condition into which they were born. At that time, not too many countries in the West yet understood this, the one exception being the US.

The second change – knowledge rather than skill

In the second place, equally important is the fact that in today's society and organizations, people work increasingly with knowledge, rather than with skill. Knowledge and skill differ in a fundamental characteristics – skills change very, very slowly.

Even today, the brocade workers in Kyoto work very much the way the inventors of silk brocades worked in the early Edo period. My ancestors started in 1517 as printers in Amsterdam in Holland - *drucker* is the Dutch word for printer. Their printing house was in existence for 250 years, until the middle of the eighteenth century. During that entire time, nothing changed in the technology of printing. My ancestor who had started in the printing shop at the age of twelve or so, the usual age for boys to go to work in those days, knew by the age of seventeen everything he needed to know to be a successful printer for the rest of his life.

Knowledge, however, changes itself. It makes itself obsolete, and very rapidly. As I have already said earlier in our dialogue, a knowledge worker becomes obsolescent if he or she does not go back to school every three or four years.

The third change – needs of 'reinventing'

In the third place, very few people lived long enough. When I was born eighty five years ago, the average life expectancy was well below fifty, even in the most advanced country, and few people who lived to that age were still fit to work. Work whether on the farm, in the craft shop, or in the factory, took a heavy toll of physical and mental health. Few people past age forty five were still capable of working full time. But life-spans have become much longer, and the working life-span has actually become even longer than the biological life-span. Working life, only a century ago, was hardly much longer than twenty or twenty five years, even though youngsters began working in their early teens. Today, we expect people to work for something like fifty years, and the demographics in all developed countries are such that we will simply not be able to support people who retire much earlier than at seventy or maybe even seventy five – provided only they are in good mental and physical health, as most people can now expect to be at that age.

This not only means that the equipment of learning, of knowledge, of skill, of experience which one acquires early, is not sufficient for our present life time and working time. People change over such a long time span. They become different persons with different needs, different abilities, different perspectives and therefore, with a need to 'reinvent themselves.' I quite intentionally use a stronger word than 'revitalize.' If you talk of fifty years of working life – and this, I think, is going to be increasingly the norm – you have to reinvent yourself. You have to make something different out of yourself, rather than just find a new supply of energy.

Balance between change and continuity

And so, I think that the questions you raise are fundamental questions, and new questions. Your questions also have a special significance for me. They are questions that have occupied my thinking almost my entire working life.

My publisher in Japan, Diamond, recently published selected essays of mine, written over the last fifty years, under the title *The Future Which Already Happened (The Ecological Vision, 1993)*. For this book, I wrote a kind of intellectual autobiography which constitutes the last chapter of the book. In it, I record the beginning of my work more than sixty years ago which was concerned with the balance between change and continuity. It was this concern that, ten years later, led me to the study of management. For I see in management, as you know, the specific organ of society that has to maintain the dynamic equilibrium between change and continuity, without which societies, organizations and individuals perish.

So, your questions are of tremendous significance to me. They are also of tremendous significance to everybody now working and living and especially to people working and living in developed societies and, therefore, in the midst of major transitions in their society, the organizations they work for, and in their own work and life.

Revitalizing oneself

Your question asks how the individual, and especially the individual who is putting knowledge to work can become effective, and how such a person can remain effective over long periods of years, over periods of change, over years of work and over years of living.

Since this question deals with the individual, it might be appropriate to start with myself. I hope you will permit me to begin by talking of seven experiences in my life which taught me how to maintain myself effective, capable of growth, capable of change – and capable of aging without becoming a prisoner of the past.

Drucker's seven experiences

I was not yet eighteen when, having finished high school, I left my native Vienna in Austria, and went to Hamburg in Germany, as a trainee in a cotton-export firm. My father was not very happy. Ours had been a family of civil servants, professors, lawyers and physicians, for a very long time. He therefore wanted me to be a full-time university student, but I was tired of being a school boy, and wanted to go to work. To appease my father, but without any serious intention, I enrolled at Hamburg University in the Law faculty. In those remote days, the year 1927, one did not have to attend classes in Austria or Germany to be a perfectly proper university student. All one had to do was to obtain signatures of the professors in the registration book. For this, one did not even have to go to class. All one had to do was to give a small tip to the faculty messenger who then went and sought the professors' signatures. There were no classes offered in the evening, and I worked during the day. During my entire year and a half in Hamburg, I therefore did not attend a single class at the university. And yet, I was considered a university student in good standing.

This sounds strange to modern ears, but it was not at least unusual in those more relaxed days. As I have recounted earlier, anyone with a high school diploma was automatically admitted to any university. All one then had to do to obtain a university degree was to pay a small annual fee and show up for an exam at the end of four years.

Work as a trainee in an export firm

The work as a trainee was terribly boring, and I learned very little. It began at seven-thirty in the morning, and was over at four in the afternoon, and at twelve on Saturday. So I had lots of free time. On weekends, two other trainees – also from Austria, but working in other firms – and I usually went hiking in the beautiful countryside outside of Hamburg, spending the night in a youth hostel where, being officially students, we could obtain free lodging. I had five week-day evenings all to myself in Hamburg's famous City Library, which was almost next door to my office. University students were encouraged to borrow as many books as they wanted. For fifteen months, I read, and read, and read, in German and English and French.

The first experience – taught by Verdi

And then, once a week, I went to the opera. The Hamburg Opera was then, as it still is, one of the world's foremost opera houses. I had very little money as trainees were not paid, but for university students, the opera was free. All one had to do was to go there one hour before the performance. Ten minutes before the performance began, cheap seats remaining unsold were given out free to university students. On one of these evenings I went to hear an opera by the great nineteenth century Italian composer, Giuseppe Verdi – the last opera he wrote in 1893, the title is *Falstaff*. It has now become one of Verdi's most popular operas, but sixty five years ago it was rarely performed. Both singers and audiences thought it too difficult. I was totally overwhelmed by it. I had a good musical education as a boy as the Vienna of my youth was an extremely musical city. Although I had heard a great many operas, I had never heard anything like this. I have never forgotten the impression that evening made on me.

'Striving for perfection' – goal and vision

When I made a study, I found, to my great surprise, that this opera, with its gaiety, its zest for life, and its incredible vitality, was written by a man aged eighty! To me, then just eighteen, eighty was an incredible age. I doubt that I even knew anyone that old. It was not a common age when life expectancies, even among healthy people, were around fifty or so. Then I read what Verdi himself had written, when he was asked why, at his age, a famous man and, considered one of the nineteenth century's foremost opera composers, he had taken on the hard work of writing one more opera, and an exceedingly demanding one. 'All my life as a musician,' he wrote, 'I have striven for perfection. It has always eluded me. I surely had an obligation to make one more try.'

I have never forgotten these words – they made an indelible impression on me. Verdi, when he was my age, that was eighteen, was of course already a seasoned musician. I had no idea what I would become, except that I knew by that time that I was unlikely to be a success exporting cotton textiles. At eighteen, I was as immature, as callow, as naive as an eighteen-year-old can be. It was not until fifteen years later, when I was in my early thirties, that I really knew what I am good at and where I belong. But I then resolved that,

103

whatever my life's work would be, Verdi's words would be my lodestar. I then resolved that if I ever reached an advanced age, I would not give up, but would keep on. In the meantime, I would strive for perfection even though, as I well knew, it would surely, always elude me.

The second experience – taught by Phidias

It was at about the same time, and also in Hamburg during my stay as a trainee, that I then read a story which conveyed to me what 'perfection' means. It is a story of the greatest sculptor of ancient Greece, Phidias. He was commissioned around 440BC to make the statues which to this day, 2400 years later, still stand on the roof of the Parthenon in Athens. To this day, they are considered among the greatest sculptures of the Western tradition. The statues were universally admired, but when Phidias submitted his bill, the City Accountant of Athens refused to pay it. 'These statues,' the accountant said, 'stand on the roof of the temple, and on the highest hill in Athens. Nobody can see anything but their fronts. Yet, you have charged us for sculpturing them in the round, that is, for doing their backsides, which nobody can see.'

'The Gods can see them'

'You are wrong,' Phidias retorted. 'The Gods can see them.' I read this, as I remember, shortly after I had listened to *Falstaff*, and it hit me hard. I have not always lived up to it. I have done many things which I hope the Gods will not notice, but I have always known that one has to strive for perfection even if only 'the Gods' notice.

Whenever people ask me which of my books I consider the best, I smile and say, 'The next.' I do not however mean it as a joke. I mean it the way Verdi meant when he talked of writing an opera at eighty in the pursuit of a perfection that had always eluded him. Though I am older now than Verdi was when he wrote *Falstaff*, I am still thinking and working on two additional books each of which, I hope, will be better than any of my earlier ones, will be more important, and will come a little closer to excellence.

Work as a journalist

A few years later, I moved to Frankfurt in Germany. I worked first as a trainee in a brokerage firm. Then after the New York

Stock Market crash in October 1929, when the brokerage firm went bankrupt, I was hired on my twentieth birthday by Frankfurt's largest newspaper, as a financial and foreign affairs writer. I continued to be enrolled as a law student at the university because in those days one could easily transfer from one European university to any other. I still was not interested in the law, but I remembered the lessons of Verdi and of Phidias. A journalist has to write about many subjects so I decided that I had to know something about many subjects to be at least a competent journalist.

The third experience – developing own method of studying

The newspaper I worked for came out in the afternoon. We began work at six in the morning and finished by a quarter-past-two in the afternoon, when the last edition went to press. So I began to force myself to study afternoons and evenings: international relations and international law; the history of social and legal institutions; history in the round; finance, and so on. Gradually, I developed a system. I still adhere to it. Every three or four years I pick a new subject. It may be statistics, it may be medieval history, it may be Japanese art, it may be economics. Three years of study are by no means enough to master a subject, but they are enough to understand it. So, for more than sixty years, I have kept on studying one subject at a time. This has not only given me a substantial fund of knowledge. It has also forced me to be open to new disciplines and new approaches and new methods – for every one of the subjects I have studied, makes different assumptions and employs a different methodology.

The fourth experience – taught by the editor-in-chief

The next experience to report in this long story of keeping myself intellectually alive and growing is what was taught by the editor-in-chief, one of Europe's leading newspapermen. The editorial staff consisted of very young people. At age twenty two, I became one of three assistant managing editors. The reason was not that I was particularly good. In fact, I never became a first-rate daily journalist. But, in those years around 1930, the people who should have held this kind of position – people aged thirty five or so – were not available in Europe. They had been killed in World War I. Even highly-responsible positions had to be filled by young people such as me. This situation was not too different from what I found in Japan when I first went there ten years after the end of the Pacific War, in the mid- and late fifties.

The editor-in-chief, then around fifty, took infinite pains to train and to discipline his young crew. He discussed with each of us every week the work we had done. Twice a year, right after New Year and then again before summer vacations began in June, we would spend a Saturday afternoon and all of Sunday to discuss our work over the preceding six months. The editor would always start out with the things we had done well. Then he would proceed to the things we had tried to do well. Next he reviewed the things where we had not tried hard enough. And finally, he would subject us to a scathing critique of the things we had done badly or had failed to do. The last two hours of that session we would then project our work for the next six months: What are the things on which we should concentrate? What are the things we should improve? What are the things each of us needs to learn? And a week later each of us was expected to submit to the editor-in-chief our new program of work and learning for the next six months.

I tremendously enjoyed the sessions, but I forgot them as soon as I left the paper.

Reviewing the preceding year

Almost ten years later, and already in the US, I remembered them. It was then in the early 1940s that I became a senior professor in a major faculty, started my own consulting practice and began to publish major books. Then I remembered what the Frankfurt editor-in-chief had taught. Since then, I have set aside two weeks every summer in which to review my work during the preceding year, beginning with the things I did well, but could or should have done better, down to the things I did poorly and the things I should have done but did not do. I decide what my priorities should be in my consulting work, in my writing, in my teaching.

I have never once truly lived up to the plan I make each August, but it has forced me to live up to Verdi's injunction 'to strive for perfection' even though 'it has always eluded me' and still does.

The fifth experience – taught by the senior partner

My next learning experience came a few years later. From Frankfurt in Germany I moved to London in England in 1933, first as a securities analyst in a large insurance company and then, a year later, to a small but fast-growing private bank as the firm's economist and executive secretary to the three senior partners – one, the founder, a man in his seventies, two others in their mid-thirties. At first I worked exclusively with the two younger men, but after I had been at the firm some three months or so, the founder called me into his office and said: 'I didn't think much of you when you came in here and still don't think much of you, but you are even more stupid than I thought you would be, and much more stupid than you have any right to be.' Since the two younger partners had been praising me to the skies each day, I was dumbfounded.

What is necessary to be effective in a new assignment

And then, the old gentleman said, 'I understand you did very good securities analysis at the insurance company. But if we had wanted you to do securities analysis work, we would have left you where you were. You are now the executive secretary to the partners yet you continue to do securities analysis. What should you be doing *now*, to be effective in your *new* job?' I was furious, but still I realized that the old man was right. I totally changed my behavior and my work. Since then, when I have a new assignment, I ask myself the question, 'What do I need to do now that I have a new assignment, to be effective?' Every time it is something different.

I have been a consultant, now, for fifty years. I have worked with many organizations and in many countries. The greatest waste of human resources in all the organizations I have seen is the failed promotion. Of able people who are being promoted and put into a new assignment, not many become true successes. Quite a few are outright failures. A very much larger number are neither successes nor failures, they become mediocrities. A handful only are successes.

The reason for sudden incompetence

Why should people who, for ten or fifteen years have been competent, suddenly become incompetent? The reason in practically all cases I have seen, is that people do what I did, sixty years ago in that London bank. They continue in their new assignment to do what made them successful in the old assignment and what earned them the promotion. Then they turn incompetent, not because they have *become* incompetent, but because they are doing the wrong things.

Requirement for success

For many years, I have made it my practice to ask those of my clients who are truly effective people – and especially those who are truly effective executives in large organizations – to what they attribute their effectiveness. Practically always, I am being told that they owe their success, as I do, to a long-dead boss, who did what the old gentleman in London did for me: force me to think through what the new assignment requires. No-one, at least not within my experience, discovers this for himself. You need someone to teach you. Once one has learned that, one does not forget it, and then – almost without exception – one is successful in the new assignment. What it requires is not superior knowledge or superior talent. It requires concentration on the things that the new assignment requires, the things that are crucial to the new challenge, the new job, the new task.

The sixth experience – taught by the Jesuits and the Calvinists

Quite a few years later, around 1945, and after I had moved from England to the US in 1937, I picked for my three-year study subject early modern European history, and especially the fifteenth and sixteenth centuries. There I found that two European institutions had become the dominant forces in Europe: The Jesuit Order in the Catholic South and the Calvinist Church in the Protestant North. Both owed their success to the same method. Both were founded independently, in 1536. Both from the very beginning adopted the same learning discipline.

Importance of writing down

Whenever a Jesuit priest or a Calvinist pastor does anything of significance, for instance, making a key decision, he is expected to write down what results he anticipates. Nine months later, he then feeds back from the actual results to these anticipations. This very soon shows him what he did well and what his strengths are. It also shows him what he has to learn and what habits he has to change. Finally it shows him what he is not gifted for and cannot do well. I have followed this method for myself now for fifty years. It brings out what one's strengths are – and this is the most important thing an individual can know about himself or herself. It brings out where improvement is needed and what kind of improvement is needed. Finally, it brings out what an individual cannot do and therefore should not even try to do. To know one's strengths, to know how to improve them, and to know what one cannot do – they are the keys to continuous learning.

The seventh experience – taught by Schumpeter

One more experience, and then I am through with the story of my personal development. At Christmas 1949 – I had just begun to teach management at New York University – my father, then seventy three years old, came to visit us from California, where he had retired a few years earlier. Right after the New Year, on January 3, 1950, he and I went to visit an old friend of his, the famous economist Joseph Schumpeter. My father had already retired, but Schumpeter, then sixty six and world-famous, was still teaching at Harvard and very active as President of the American Economic Association.

In 1902 my father was a young civil servant in the Austrian Ministry of Finance, but also did some teaching in economics at the university. He had come to know Schumpeter, then at age nineteen, the most brilliant of the young students. Two more different people are hard to imagine: Schumpeter was flamboyant, arrogant, abrasive, and vain; my father, quiet, the soul of courtesy and modest to the point of being self-effacing. Still the two became fast friends and remained fast friends.

By 1949, Schumpeter had become a very different person. Sixty six years old and in his last year of teaching at Harvard, he was at the peak of his fame. The two old men had a wonderful time together reminiscing about the old days. Both had grown up and had worked in Austria, and both had eventually come to America, Schumpeter in 1932 and my father, four years later. Suddenly, my father asked with a chuckle: 'Joseph, do you still talk about what you want to be remembered for?' Schumpeter broke out in loud laughter, and even I laughed. For Schumpeter was notorious for having said, when he was thirty or so and had published the first two of his great economic books, that what he really wanted to be remembered for was to have been 'Europe's greatest lover of beautiful women, and Europe's greatest horseman – and perhaps also as the world's greatest economist.' Schumpeter said, 'Yes, this question is still important to me, but I now answer it differently. I want to be remembered as having been the teacher who converted half a dozen brilliant students into first-rate economists.

He must have seen an amazed look on my father's face because he continued,, 'You know, Adolph, I have now reached the age where I know that being remembered for books and theories is not enough. One does not make a difference unless it is a difference in the lives of people.' One reason my father had gone to see Schumpeter was that it was known that he was very sick and would not live long. Schumpeter died five days after we had visited him.

I have never forgotten that conversation. I have learned from it three things. First, one has to ask oneself what one wants to be remembered for. Secondly, that should change as one gets older. It should change both with one's own maturity and with the changes in the world. Finally, one thing worth being remembered for is the difference one makes in the lives of people.

The same things are learned by successful people

I am telling this long story for a simple reason. All the people I know who have managed to remain effective during a long life, have learned pretty much the same things I learned. This applies to effective business executives and to scholars; to top-ranking military people and to first-rate physicians; to teachers and to artists. Whenever I work with a person, and as a consultant I have been working of course with a great many, in businesses, in governments, in universities, in hospitals, in opera houses, in symphony orchestras, in museums, and so on I sooner or later try to find out to what the individual attributes his or her success. I am invariably told stories that are remarkably like mine.

Doing a few simple things

And so, to answer to the question, 'How can the individual, and especially the individual in knowledge work maintain his or her effectiveness?' would be: 'By doing a few fairly simple things.'

The first one is to have the kind of goal or vision which Verdi's *Falstaff* gave me. To keep on striving means that one matures but one does not age.

Secondly, I have found that the people who maintain their effectiveness take the view Phidias took of his own work: the Gods see it. They are not willing to do work that is only average. They have respect for the integrity of their work. In fact, they have self-respect.

The third thing these people all have in common: they build continuous learning into the way they live. They may not do what I have been doing for more than sixty years now, that is, to become a student of a new discipline every three or four years. They experiment. They are not satisfied with doing what they did yesterday. The very least they demand of themselves is that they do better, whatever they do, and more often, they demand of themselves that they do it differently.

The people who keep themselves alive and growing also build a review of their performance into their work. An increasing number, I have found, do what the Jesuits and Calvinists of the sixteenth century first thought of. They keep a record of the results of their actions and decisions, and compare them with their expectations. Then they soon know what their strengths are, but they also know what they have to improve, to change, to learn. Finally they know what they are not good at, and what they therefore should let other people do.

Again and again, when I ask one of these effective people to tell me the experiences that explains their success, I hear that a long-dead teacher or a boss challenged them and taught them that whenever one changes one's work, one's position, one's assignment, one thinks through what the new job, the new position, the new assignment requires. Always it requires something different from what the preceding job or the preceding assignment required.

Responsibility for one's own development and placement

The most important thing that underlies all these practices is that individuals, and especially knowledge people, who manage to keep themselves effective, and who manage to keep on growing and changing, take responsibility for their development and their placement.

This may be the most novel conclusion. And it may be the one which is most difficult to apply in Japan. Today's organization, whether it is a business, or a government agency, is still based on the assumption that the organization is responsible for placing the individual and for providing the experiences and challenges that the individual needs. The best example of this I know is the personnel department in the typical, large Japanese company, or the prototype on which it has been modelled, or the personnel department in a traditional army. I know no more responsible group of people than those in the typical Japanese personnel department. Yet they will, I think, have to learn to change. Instead of being decision-makers they will have to become teachers, guides, counselors, advisors. The responsibility for the development of the individual knowledge worker, and for his or her placement, will, I am convinced, have to be taken by the individual. It will have to become very much the responsibility of the individual to ask: What kind of assignment do I now need? What kind of assignment am I now qualified for? What kind of experience and what kind of knowledge and skill do I now need to acquire? The decision of course, cannot be that of the individual alone. It has to be made in contemplation of the needs of the organization. It also has to be made on the basis of an outside appraisal of the strengths, the competencies, the performance of the individual.

Responsibility for development of the individual has to become responsibility for self-development. Responsibility for placing the individual has to become the responsibility for self-placement. Otherwise, it is unlikely that knowledge people can continue to remain effective and productive and capable of growth over the long span of working-life we can now expect.

January 12, 1995

Executives can affect people's lives
Isao Nakauchi

IN YOUR REPLY, YOU DESCRIBED your personal experiences. These revealled some of the secrets of your many active years at the front-line, and I am impressed by your drive constantly to improve yourself.

You explained that anyone can produce similar results by following five simple principles: (1) set yourself targets or goals; (2) be proud of your work and take it seriously; (3) strive to learn continually in your daily life; (4) discover your strengths by making self-evaluation a part of your work; and (5) apply yourself diligently to new work, new roles and new duties. While these are certainly simple and worthwhile rules that can readily be put into practice, maintaining the momentum is not so easy. It requires patience and effort. That you have been able to sustain these principles over many years is a credit to you.

As far as ordinary people are concerned, your views are both highly considerate and very strict. This strictness, though, is required of the citizens of industrialized countries, who have a responsibility to the entire world. These days, although private enterprise may espouse change, company employees are less likely to be thinking about what they can do at work to benefit society. Employees increasingly expect the company to look after their lives, satisfied that all will be well if they just follow orders correctly. You have harsh words indeed for these people. Each and every one of us must take heed of your words: 'Individuals, and especially knowledge people, who manage to keep themselves effective and who manage to keep on growing and changing, take responsibility for development.'

Responsibility of executives

As you point out, Professor Drucker, we cannot simply rely on personnel training and study programs to revitalize ordinary people. The only way is to instill a sense of self-responsibility. For some time now I have sensed this to be true. Now your words have given me a sense of legitimacy and strengthened my resolve. As you say, in order to make each and every employee aware of the significance of self-responsibility, personnel officers must move away from being deci-

113

sion-makers, and assume the role of personal tutors to every employee, advisors on career paths, consultants and counsellors.

Reading your letter again brought home to me your excellent sense of proportion. While calling for greater efforts from ordinary people, you also mention the responsibilities of executives, as related through the conversation between your father and Schumpeter.

You quoted Schumpeter as saying: 'One does not make a difference unless it is a difference in the lives of people.' I interpret this to mean that one cannot be called an executive unless one is able to make a difference in the lives of people. The words of Schumpeter should provide food for thought for these executives at maj or companies who see themselves simply as administrators. An executive is more than an administrator. He or she must be an educated person, capable of managing organizational change to achieve continuing stability. In this sense, to become an executive and remain an executive, one must not rely on the company but take responsibility for one's own continued learning and development process, just as for ordinary people. Like Verdi, who wrote an opera at the age of eighty in an ongoing quest for perfection; like Phidias, the sculptor who knew that 'the Gods' could see what others could not; and like yourself, we must constantly strive for perfection in all that we do.

The Nakauchi experiences

I must tell you that reading your letter made me realize that, as an executive, I, too, must strive for this goal, indeed that there is no other alternative. Your experiences have also prompted me to look back over my own life and reflect on my thoughts and deeds.

My experience as a business manager, while certainly not as illustrious as your own, can be characterized as a continuous learning process.

On 23 September 1957, during the oppressive lingering heat of summer, I opened my first store in Senbayashi, Osaka, selling drugs, cosmetics, canned and bottled goods and everyday articles. This small, 97-square meter shop represents the first ever Daiei outlet. Senbayashi, one of the few areas in Osaka to escape devastation during the war, was transformed into a major shopping precinct during the late 1950s. The new Daiei store was to be situated in the middle of this precinct and right in front of the railway station.

Despite the good location, not one business was performing well, prompting the land owner to consider converting into warehouses. Passers-by, upon seeing preparations underway for the Daiei store, would just shake their heads. As the opening drew near, rumors spread that our store would offer incredibly low prices, attracting interest from local residents and travellers using the nearby station. We announced the store opening using leaflets inserted in newspapers, giving product names but not prices; this strategy may well have contributed to our success.

We were deluged with customers from the early morning of the very first day. Takings on the first day were 280,000 yen, far beyond the 60,000 yen we had calculated as the break-even point. All thirteen employees were exhausted but thrilled at the outcome.

Asking customers' needs

But our euphoria was not to continue for long. A competitor opened just nearby on the fourth day and daily takings fell to around 20,000 yen. We tried various methods to draw in customers, such as hanging leaflets in the front of the store, but to no avail. Once again, people began saying that any store in our area was eventually destined for failure. We resolved to ask a wide range of customers what products they would like to see the store. As a result, it was decided to put sweets in the shop front.

Although it is hard to imagine nowadays, Japan then was very poor, with little in the way of amusement or entertainment. Back in those days, virtually the only form of entertainment was to visit friends who owned a television (black-and-white, naturally) and eat sweets while watching the programs. This had been revealed through our inquiries, so we concluded that sweets would sell well. We resolved to provide sweets at the front of our store, selling by weight as was the norm at that time.

This proved an instant success. For days on end, the store was in turmoil, but the inherently slow method of selling by weight had created a new problem. We were simply unable to cope with the flow during peak periods. The staff did everything they could to speed up the process; after closing time, for instance, they would practice putting standard amounts into a bag, but this was not enough to keep up with demand.

A little innovation

Clearly, some sort of revolutionary new technique was required. After much thought, we hit upon the answer: sweets would be measured out and pre-packed into polyethylene bags, which had just become available. This broke with traditional convention. The age of pre-packing had arrived.

At that time, tasting constituted the principal reason for purchasing by weight. Customers could try sweets for free before they actually bought them. They were unsure about the pre-packed sweets, worrying that the taste and flavor would not be the same as the samples. Some even refused to buy our 'flavorless' offerings without tasting. So we offered them a money-back guarantee if they were dissatisfied. We appealed to our customers to trust us not to sell inferior goods. It was said that our pre-packed sweets would quickly be stolen, but we had faith in our customers. We had enough faith in our customers so that if the business did collapse, it would be our fault in that we had failed to win their trust. Indeed, if that were the case then we fully deserved to collapse. We reasoned that if customers really wanted what we were providing, then they would accept any kind of method and support us.

As it turned out, our revolutionary sales technique did in fact win the trust and support of consumers throughout Japan. Within six months of the initial opening, Daiei takings had passed the million yen per day mark, disproving the prevailing wisdom that success was impossible in our part of town.

A new store in Sannomiya, Kobe

The next Daiei store opened on 2 December 1958 in Kobe's Sannomiya district, an area where I was raised as a child and which has sustained considerable damage in the recent earthquake. It was just over one year after the Senbayashi store began trading.

A single leaflet was the only advertising undertaken prior to opening. Yet our reputation must have spread from Osaka as far as Kobe, for the town was full of talk about the incredibly cheap store soon to open.

Sannomiya at that time was a run-down area where shanty

houses jostled together with outdoor drinking stalls and cheap food halls, primarily for day workers. It was not a place frequented by women and children during the day, let alone in the evening. The new Daiei store, however, brought women with shopping baskets to the streets of Sannomiya in search of cheap goods. From the very first day, the store was packed with shoppers between ten in the morning and eight at night. The staff had not a moment's proper rest. They had to take turns to dash to the nearest noodle shop for lunch, eating their meal standing since there was no time to wait for a seat.

With the Sannomiya store about to burst, we decided to move operations to a two-story wooden structure with more than twice the floor space, just a hundred meters away. The new store began trading on 25 April 1959, five months after its predecessor. This was to become the focus of Daiei activities in the ensuring years and the first step in our expansion as a chain store. Customers were attracted to the new store by the fluorescent lighting and self-service shelf display setup, which were revolutionary at the time though they are now standard practice.

Beef for 39 yen

The main attraction, the thing that really amazed shoppers, was our offer of 100 grams of beef for just 39 yen. This particular product played a major role in building Daiei's reputation as the place to buy meat, and is something that I will never forget.

As Japan finally began to regain her energy at the end of the 1950s, people were able to eat decent meals again. At last the nation was taking off, heading towards the advanced mass consumer society envisaged in the Income-Doubling Plan proposed by the government of Ikeda Hayato in 1960. This atmosphere triggered an escalating demand for beef, previously considered a luxury item.

In light of these changes, it was clear to me that beef was going to play an increasingly large role in the dietary patterns of Japanese consumers. I set out to challenge the accepted wisdom that only experts could sell beef, by selling at 39 yen per 100 grams instead of the 60 yen charged by butchers. The reaction was incredible. The meat section was literally swamped day after day, to the point where we had to set up a temporary sales counter on a neighboring lot next door in order to keep up with demand.

Cessation of supplies

Nearby meat sellers reacted by forcing our wholesale suppliers to cease working with us. Sales plummeted as a result. I was at a loss. We even tried buying livestock and paying to have them slaughtered and dressed, but the losses were too great. In order to retain the faith of our customers and extricate ourselves from the deadlock, it would be necessary to obtain large volumes of meat through a different route, so that we could continue to provide cheaply. People spoke of the end for Daiei, but I resolved to fight on. I introduced myself to each wholesaler in turn, asking them to sell to us, but my efforts seemed fruitless, no doubt because of the pressure from our butchers. I was ignored by the wholesalers.

Finally I came across a wholesaler willing to sell meat to 'the Daiei that everyone was talking about.' I had found an angel in the midst of hell! Following negotiations conducted in the freezer, some twenty or thirty degrees below zero, I signed a contract for the seven carcasses hanging in front of my eyes. The helping hand of this wholesaler, who was prepared to forfeit eight of his regular customers to do business with me, enabled Daiei to weather the crisis and revived our sales at the meat counter.

As sales increased, we went on to solicit meat from as far away as Kagoshima, Okinawa and even Australia, changing our sales methods in the process.

Sales of packed meat

At that time, the standard one-on-one approach involved slicing the meat according to the customer's instructions. Ours was the first attempt at self-service meat in Japan. Since the equipment and materials, such as the scales and trays required for self-service, were not adequate back in around 1964, it was more time-consuming to produce pre-packed meat than to sell individually to customers, who were also deeply suspicious of the packed meat.

However, I knew that self-service, with its low personnel expenses, was the only way to satisfy the demand for large quantities of high-quality meat at low cost. New employees were sent to Hawaii right after joining to compare and try various different sales techniques, both domestic and foreign. Our meat counters changed under their influence and, slowly but surely, suspicion of packed meat wore off and self-serv-

ice began to gain popularity. The process continued to the
extent that individual meat retailing is now a rarity. I believe
that the efforts of our young staff, coupled with Daiei's role
as an organization, started off the conversion to self-service
meat, now available in stores throughout Japan.

Orange juice and the strategy of low pricing

Another experience I should like to discuss here is also the
most recent. With the 1992 liberalization of orange juice imports to Japan, Daiei brought out its own brand orange juice
that boasts no changes in physical composition whatsoever.
We had created a new product simply by selling an existing
product at way below the city price.

Though it may seem unimaginable, orange juice in 1992 cost
above three dollars for a one-liter pack, and was marketed as
a special drink, for instance, that one might serve to guests at
home. A questionnaire survey conducted at retail outlets revealed that, on the contrary, Japanese consumers saw orange
juice as an ordinary beverage on a par with milk. We reasoned that orange juice costing about the same as milk (just
under $2.00 per liter in Japan) would satisfy the demand of,
say, consumers who wanted to be able to drink orange juice
every morning at breakfast. To achieve this, we reevaluated
all the costs involved, from the raw material imported through
to the final processing. Production and distribution costs were
reduced by importing lower cost ingredients from Brazil and
processing in large quantities at a limited number of plants.
Promotion costs were also reduced by selling under the Daiei
brand name.

The result is that Daiei orange juice costs 30-40 per cent less
than similar products on the market. It is extremely popular
with consumers, so much so that sales are already well over
the target levels. Prices of existing national brands have been
forced down, and the media have dubbed our orange juice
the pioneer of the phenomenon known as 'price destruction'
in Japan. Personally, I didn't try to be violent in 'destroying,'
pointing out that we have merely done our best to satisfy
customer demand. In this sense, it would not be an exaggeration to say that our orange juice is a revolutionary product that changed the economic fabric of Japan.

The first lesson – 'Innovation means parting with convention'

Professor Drucker, hearing of your experiences and subsequently looking back on my own has taught me three important lessons.

Firstly, innovation means parting with the conventional wisdom, overhauling one's existing work from the ground up. Pre-packed sweets at our store in Senbayashi, meat at low prices in Sannomiya, and then pre-packed meat, each of these flew in the face of conventional practices at the time. In the end, the overwhelming level of consumer support that we gained formed the foundations for Daiei as it is today.

Similarly, we achieved our vision of 'low-price orange juice for the breakfast table' through a complete overhaul of existing processes to cut costs, searching out new suppliers of raw ingredients and taking a new approach to manufacturing.

My experiences demonstrate that innovation is not possible while one remains trapped within the hard shell of conventional wisdom, and further, that innovation is not a lofty ideal, but something that can be triggered by even the tiniest change.

During my visits to stores, I often have cause to feel that fewer and fewer employees these days are imbued with the spirit of innovation. Daiei is not the only one losing its climate of innovation. As noted in your letter, the problem is common to all major Japanese enterprises. Many guides to business management have been published in an attempt to solve the problem, but I believe that the most important thing is to enable people actually to experience innovation for themselves. For this reason, I want as many Daiei employees and others to read about my experiences, as described in this letter, in order to reaffirm the importance of innovation, to realize that it can be triggered by even the tiniest change. I sincerely hope that this will serve as the driving force for more young people to experience and produce innovation for themselves.

The second lesson – importance of adopting the perspective of the consumer

The second thing I have learned is the importance of always striving to adopt the perspective of the consumer, of the masses.

Putting sweets in bags was an emergency strategy tailored to suit the average Japanese lifestyle at the time. If we had confined ourselves to being a drugstore, if we had not considered the non-customers of which you talk, if we had continued to serve only sick people (constituting an extremely limited market) then we might well have given up the fight with our competitors, lost our corporate strength and eventually would have fallen into bankruptcy. Daiei escaped this fate by listening to our customers, focusing our efforts on sweets, a central part of everyday life for most people, and providing these in inexpensive, pre-packed form. Similarly, it was the overwhelming support of our customers that enabled us to bring back supplies of meat at 39 yen per 100 grams to stores following the suspension of deliveries. It was their support that took me to the wholesalers' shops, found me face to face with a willing trader and kept me going during sub-zero temperature negotiations in the freezer.

At the height of the bubble economy period in Japan, there was much speculation on the alleged disappearance of 'the masses.' The orange juice experience demonstrates, however, that there are still many products capable of winning their support. This represents a major opportunity for Daiei.

The third lesson – corporate philosophy and continuous learning

At last, I have realized the importance of incorporating continuous learning into the work process, as you already stressed. Looking back, I believe that my experiences demonstrate a part of that which is required of an executive.

At our Sannomiya store, I wanted to apply our corporate philosophy – better goods at lower prices and an affluent life style for the customers – to meat sales and told our younger employees to reevaluate the meat section accordingly. As a result of their own efforts to study and learn and their determined efforts to incorporate creative new ideas, we succeeded in remodelling the meat counter and introducing self-service operations. This demonstrates that if we want to bring life to organizations and employees, we have to elucidate the corporate philosophy from the outset, and then encourage the employees themselves to study widely and to incorporate their own creative ideas and proposals into everyday work, in line with the philosophy. Surely, then, it is the responsibility of executives to create an environment that encourages continuous self-learning by ordinary people and the use of creative ideas and proposals.

Professor Drucker, my experiences are certainly not as illustrious as yours. Nevertheless, I believe that the path I have taken, shedding sweat and tears along with my workers, has made me who I am today. And more than anything else, the support of the consumers has given me the strength to carry on, and enabled me to turn Daiei into a large corporate group. Consumers will continue to exist, and Daiei will continue striving to meet their expectations. Our mission is one of continually striving to be better. To realize this, I pledge to you to redouble my efforts in continuing learning and growth, so that my best business decision is the next one.

February 25, 1995

7

Reinventing business

How to design an organization structure that can revitalize a company?
Isao Nakauchi

Responsibility of corporations

It is often said that recently, with the development of information technology, particularly within American corporations, it has become common for remote employees to have direct dialogues with top management executives using e-mail. Furthermore, it is also said that such corporations are organized more as flat, network structures and not traditional, vertical hierarchies, and outsourcing has now become a natural part of business in Japan as well.

In this way, as organizations become lateral and outsourcing becomes common, just as the Japanese mass media and many think-tanks are explaining, the need for middle-level managers in a vertical, hierarchical organization will disappear. However, those men and women are living human beings. Simply because they are no longer needed, we cannot just lay them off. Rather, it is an important responsibility of executives to give those people opportunities. This situation obviously presents a big dilemma for corporations. As organizations are made lateral and outsourcing becoming a common practice, is it still possible to continue to give exciting opportunities to the middle management without large layoffs? In your work, 'The Delusion of Profits' in *The Future Which Has Already Happened*, you stated, 'Generating the profit necessary to cover the cost of today's employment and tomorrow's employment is a socioeconomic responsibility of the corporation.' What should corporations do so that such a responsibility can be fulfilled?

I would appreciate some specific examples of how you design an organization convenient for managers, that incorporates profitable organizational aspects, that can cover the cost of employment, and that aims at investment for tomorrow.

January 9, 1995

Without an effective mission statement, there will be no performance
Peter Drucker

The short life-span of the business enterprise

Organizations are human creations and, as such, neither infallible nor immortal. Of all organizations, business enterprise is both the one that is most prone to error, and has the shortest life-span. For business enterprise, by definition and alone among all major organizations of society, is the change-agent. All other structures are basically created to conserve and to perpetuate. Business enterprise, alone, is created both to exploit change in economy and society, and to create change in economy and society. This makes it, by definition, a far riskier venture than any other major organization. It also means that it much sooner accomplishes its purpose, if managed superbly well, and will therefore, much sooner than any other institution, disappear or at least become ineffectual. All human institutions need to balance continuity and change, but in business enterprise, that challenge is ever-present.

The need to change the university

Other major organizations need to change, too, but much less often. The modern university, for instance, was created almost two hundred years ago in 1809, with the foundation of the University of Berlin amidst the turmoil of the Napoleonic Wars. For almost two hundred years, the university has remained fundamentally unchanged. We have added to it, have patched here and mended there. We have created new additional institutions, such as the technical university and the business school, but we have not fundamentally had to change the university's design. Only now, two centuries after its original creation, is it becoming necessary – and rapidly so – to think through again what is the purpose of the university, what is its mission, what should be its structure, and so on.

The need to change government

Government, too, needs change. In fact, without the ability to change, government degenerates. There have been literally hundreds of constitutions since the ancient Athenians wrote the first one 2600 years ago. None of these constitutions survived more than a few short years, at most three or four decades. The American Constitution has now survived for two hundred years, something for which there is no precedent in history. It owes its survival to the fact that the Founding Fathers wrote into it provisions for its being changed, and also created in the Supreme Court, an organ specifically designed to adapt the Constitution to changes in society, economy and technology. However, it is only now, two hundred years after the United States was first founded on a written constitution, that the need to think through the function of government is coming to the fore, as will be discussed a little later in this dialogue.

Victims of success

Very few businesses can prosper even five or seven years without substantial change and massive rethinking of the very concepts on which they are based. There are exceptions, to be sure, but they are rare. It is by no means sure that it is a blessing for a business to enjoy long decades of continuity without challenge to its fundamental concepts and assumptions. There is an old Chinese proverb: 'Whom the gods want to destroy, they give forty years of success.' Business history amply proves the wisdom of this old saying.

There are a few businesses around with a basic theory that goes back a century. There is the universal bank (founded almost simultaneously around 1870 in Germany and in Japan) and the *zaibatsu* invented by Mitsubishi (and reborn after World War II as *keiretsu*). Both concepts are clearly in crisis today, and are rapidly losing their effectiveness.

In the US, the four most successful businesses of this century were, respectively, the Bell Telephone System (AT&T), which alone, of all major telephone systems in the world remained privately-owned and did not become nationalized; Sears Roebuck, for almost half a century the world's most successful retailer; General Motors; and IBM. The Bell Telephone System was conceived and designed around 1910 when its predecessor was on the verge of bankruptcy. Sears Roebuck, as it came to dominate the American retail scene, was designed in the early 1920s, as was General Motors. And IBM was designed right after World War II. For seventy years, the Bell Telephone System knew nothing but growth and success. For more than fifty years, Sears Roebuck and General Motors knew nothing but growth and success. For forty years, IBM knew nothing but growth and success. All four looked invincible, but when the time came for them to change, they proved impotent and ineffectual. They became the victims of their own success.

Fortune's top 500 companies

Businesses that go unchallenged for long decades are rare exceptions. The great majority, no matter how successful, need to think through their basic assumptions much sooner. The great majority, moreover, then find it almost impossible to change. The business which, after ten years of continuing success, retains the capacity to change and to maintain its effectiveness, is in the minority. It may not disappear, but it is likely to become an 'also ran' and to fall way behind.

The American magazine *Fortune* has for more than forty years published each year a list of the 500 top manufacturing companies in the US. During these forty years, one-third of the companies in the original list have disappeared from it altogether – either because they have been liquidated or merged or because they have become insignificant. Another third has lost position in the list, that is, has dropped from being a major to become a relatively minor business. Only one-third have maintained themselves in the list, that is, in their position in the American economy.

The threat of continuing success

Every one of these companies that has been able to prosper for four decades has had to change fundamentally. Yet, the last forty years have been years of great continuity and, generally, years of tremendous prosperity, not only in the American economy but in the world economy.

What is needed is not only the capacity to overcome adversity. Equally important, and equally needed, is the capacity to take advantage of opportunity, and this, too, is equally threatened by continuing success, threatened by complacency.

An example of an automobile company

The best examples are recent ones. One is the recent inability of the world's most successful automobile companies to see, let alone to take advantage of, the sharp shift on the part of the American automobile buyer to sports-utility vehicles, mini-vans and pick-up trucks. General Motors should have been the foremost beneficiary.

For when the shift began, in the early 1980s, General Motors had by far the best-designed vehicles of this kind, enjoyed the best reputation in the market, and had the lowest production costs. Yet, General Motors simply missed the market. Sports-utility vehicles, mini-vans and pick-up trucks were not considered 'passenger cars' and were not included as such in the monthly statistics of automobile sales. No-one in General Motors' top management fifteen years ago, therefore, even realized that these 'non-passenger cars' were where the market was growing.

But Toyota and Nissan equally missed this opportunity. By the late 1980s, the Japanese-made automobile had established itself in the American market as the market leader and as the quality standard. It seemed to be invincible. Again, because sports-utility vehicles, mini-vans and pick-up trucks were not classified as 'passenger vehicles', the Japanese missed the market shift in the US just as much as General Motors did.

The opportunity was exploited by the two weaker American automobile companies, Ford and Chrysler, both of which in the mid-1980s, seemed totally unable to compete against either the Japanese or their much bigger American rival. This explains, by the way, why in the last five years neither General Motors nor the Japanese have been able to grow in the American market – three have been losing ground steadily. Even though all three now have the right products on the market, the three are still steadily losing market share in the American automobile market. What is probably more important, they are steadily losing their leadership image.

It is, thus, no accident that the management literature has increasingly concerned itself with the management of change and with revitalizing business enterprise. The first book on these subjects was probably my work *Managing For Results* in 1964.

Mission and its importance

The management of change is, however, the wrong place to start. What has to come first is the management of continuity. Every business enterprise needs to balance continuity and change, and that has to begin with establishing the fundamental direction, that is, with the continuity of the enterprise. To make a business effective does indeed require that it be able to use change as an opportunity, but this, in turn, requires first that the enterprise have a clear mission. The present discussion of the management of change often forgets this. Without such a mission – that is, without continuity – the enterprise is rudderless and only drifts.

The role of the mission statement

Mr Nakauchi's statement that the mission of Daiei is 'to halve the price of commodities by the year 2010' sounds deceptively simple. All effective mission statements do. Yet, like all effective mission statements, it is a call to action rather than pious intention. It tells the people in the company what their values are, and what effectiveness means for the company and for their own work. Like all effective mission statements, it makes a team out of what otherwise would be a mob, with each employee doing his or her own work rather than focusing on a common purpose. Without an effective mission statement, in other words, there will be no performance.

As is the case with Daiei, the effective mission statement is not a statement of financial goals. They flow from effective performance. The mission statement has to express the contribution the enterprise plans to make to society, to economy, to the customer. It has to express the fact that the business enterprise is an institution of society and serves to produce social benefits.

Financial results are not the purpose

Mission statements that express the purpose of the enterprise in financial terms fail inevitably, to create the cohesion, the dedication, the vision of the people who have to do the work so as to realize the enterprise's goal.

An old saying – going back to ancient Rome, I believe – states that 'Human beings eat to live, but do not live to eat.' Similarly, enterprises have to have satisfactory financial results to live; without them they cannot survive and cannot, in fact, do their job. However, they do not exist to have financial results. Financial results, by themselves, are not adequate, are not the purpose of the enterprise, and are not the justification and reason for its existence.

Competitive cost of living

Implicit in every effective mission statement are clear assumptions regarding the reality in which the enterprise works. In the case of Daiei's, I imagine that one underlying assumption is the reality of an increasingly borderless world. One implication of this is that Japan, in order to be able to compete, must not have higher cost than other developed countries. The first costs in any economy are not wages. They are what wages buy, that is, the cost of living. In that respect, Japan today is not competitive, as you, Mr Nakauchi, have been pointing out for years. Therefore, the basic assumption underlying Daiei's mission statement is that Japan's cost of living has to become competitive, and this is what Daiei is going to bring about. This is what you mean when you talk about the 'distribution revolution.'

A second implication of the reality of a borderless world is that Daiei – and any other retailer with whom Daiei competes, whether in Japan or in the US – can and must procure commodities where they can be bought at the lowest price and the highest quality. This, too, clearly implies a challenge to the present Japanese reality.

A true merchant

Finally, the Daiei statement, like any effective mission statement, makes clear what core competencies the company must have to carry out its mission. It has to be a truly outstanding merchant – and a merchant is not someone who sells. A merchant is someone who buys for his customers.

Ability to convert change into opportunity

I have gone into such lengths to discuss the Daiei mission statement for the simple reason that very few businessmen truly understand the importance of a clear mission statement such as Daiei has, and the implications of that mission statement. Yet, unless there is such clarity, change cannot be managed. Unless there is such clarity, the executive will not be able to convert change – whether in economy, in technology, in society – into business opportunities. But the ultimate test of management is its ability to do just that. The ultimate test is not to be able to survive and to be able to cope with change as a threat. The ultimate test of management is the ability to make change serve the mission of the enterprise – to manage change as an opportunity.

Welcoming change

To do this, the first requirement is to build organized abandonment into the business. It is to be able to keep the enterprise – no matter how big – lean, flexible, and eager to do new things. There is a great deal of talk today about overcoming 'resistance to change'. However, to be able to take advantage of change, enterprises have to welcome change. They have to consider change as normal rather than as an exception to be feared and to be avoided if at all possible. They have to be innovative, in other words. This requires that the enterprise is organized systematically to abandon the outworn and obsolete; to get rid of things that do not work, no matter how attractive they looked when the enterprise first went into them; to concentrate resources, especially of competent people, on opportunities, rather than waste them on yesterday's problems; and to work together on developing tomorrow rather than on defending yesterday.

Organized abandonment

The first requirement for keeping an enterprise vital and effective is to build into it a systematic policy which subjects every three or four years each product and service, and each policy and procedure, to the question: 'If we did not already do this, would we now, knowing what we now know, go into it?' The answer is rarely an unqualified 'Yes.' It is often 'Yes – but we have learned a few things and are now going to do this differently.' The answer, equally often, will be 'No.' Then one asks: 'What do we do now?' Maybe all that is needed is to reposition a business, a product, a service. Maybe it needs to be redesigned. Maybe it needs to be abandoned. But unless the enterprise subjects itself to the discipline of organized abandonment, it will not be able to tackle the new.

'Five Deadly Business Sins'

Without an organized policy of abandonment, enterprises will always feed problems and starve opportunities. This is the first of what I call the 'Five Deadly Business Sins' – and far too many companies indulge in all five. To be able to remain effective and to manage change and opportunity, however, the other four – numbers 2 through 5 – have to be avoided, too. Number 2 – particularly common in American, but also in European business – is the worship of high profit margins and of 'premium pricing.' This only benefits the competitor. Then – number 3 – there is the common sin of mispricing a new product or a new service by pricing it at 'what the market will bear,' rather than pricing it on what will create the largest demand, and will satisfy the largest numbers of customers. Mispricing a product also, in the end, benefits the competitor. Pricing that is based on one's costs rather than price-driven costing is the next – number 4 – of the deadly business sins. An effective company starts out with the price that is optimal for the market and then works back to what the costs must be, so that the product or the service can be offered at that price. This, by the way, is the lesson which the Japanese have taught us in the US and in Europe these last ten or fifteen years. For price-driven costing, to a large extent, underlies the success of the Japanese in the West. Finally – number 5 – there is the common sin of slaughtering tomorrow's opportunity at the altar of yesterday. It is the sin that underlies the decline of IBM. It subordinated the new and growing personal computer to the maintenance of the old and declining product, the large mainframe computer.

System for organized innovation

Of course, to remain effective and to be able to exploit change as an opportunity, it is not enough for a business not to do the wrong things. It has to build organized innovation into its system. It has to work systematically on looking for change inside and outside. I have discussed methods of doing this at considerable length in a book that is now ten years old, *Innovation and Entrepreneurship*. Businesses stay ahead of competition and both attain and maintain leadership by systematically looking for changes that have already occurred inside and outside, and asking, 'Is this change an opportunity?' The change may be in an unexpected success or an unexpected failure. It may be in demographics. It may, like the

131

change on which Daiei has based so much of its growth, be in fundamental changes in world economy, in information and in world politics. It may be in technology – and this, too, is an area which Daiei has used as an opportunity for successful innovation. What is important is that this search for opportunity is done systematically, and permeates the entire organization, which also means that it has to be built into the personnel policy of the organization and its incentives, encouragement, and rewards.

Concept of mission

This is, of course, nothing but the merest sketch of a very big subject, but it should suffice to show that we know how to maintain the vitality of a business. It does not lie in reacting to change. It lies in renewing oneself continuously, by using change as an opportunity. But this will work only, I repeat, if the enterprise is also managed for continuity, and has at its foundation a clear concept of its mission and of its purpose in society and economy.

January 12, 1995

The very reason for the existence of a company is to turn what is learned immediately into action, thus contributing to society
Isao Nakauchi

The customer determines the price

Of particular interest to me is your argument that setting prices based on existing costs, a principle still firmly entrenched in manufacturing and other industries, constitutes one of the five deadly sins of private enterprise. Instead, you maintain that all necessary costs should be calculated backwards from the price sought by the customer. I am pleased to note that this is wholly consistent with the approach that Daiei has taken ever since its founding: the customer determines the price.

I also appreciate your words of praise ('a management philosophy destined to produce results') for Daiei's simple philosophy – better goods at lower prices and an affluent lifestyle for the customers – the goal being 'to cut prices by half.'

You replied that to make a business effective requires the ability to use social change as an opportunity. Your subsequent comments on Daiei's management philosophy were very accurate.

The Daiei corporate ideal of 'better goods at lower prices and an affluent life-style for the customers' has remained unchanged since the company's founding. This means exactly what it says, nothing more and nothing less.

A continuous program of training is required to enable employees to ascertain what the customer really wants, and to convert the results into action immediately. To learn constantly, and immediately to turn what we have learned into reality, thereby contributing to society, constitutes the very reason for Daiei's existence.

Unfortunately, I must say that I have had an occasion recently to feel that it might be more appropriate to say that this used to constitute the very reason for Daiei's existence. More than weathered principles, the notion of cutting prices by half represents a specific goal. As you pointed out, this provides the impetus for action. Similarly, our target of cutting prices by half calls for all employees to think from the customer's perspective, both realistically and rationally, about how he or she can help to achieve this goal. That is the reason I say 'prices will be cut by half' if we take action, instead of 'we will cut price by half.'

February 25, 1995

8

Reinventing society

Converting organizations into social entities that
contribute to society can protect society from
degeneration
Isao Nakauchi

Destiny of advanced nations

Many great and historical economists have predicted a dark
scenario on the destiny of capitalism. Specifically, Adam Smith
spoke of the saturation of demand and the degeneration of
the labor force, Karl Marx of the alienation of the working
class, Keynes of persistent underemployment, and
Schumpeter of the degeneration and end of culture. Each
time I think about the hidden meaning in these words which
have been passed down to us, I believe that Japan, and all
advanced nations, will head down the same path of destiny
as the Roman Empire, which, as a result of its affluence,
triumphed to its destruction.

However, we, the responsible executives of the advanced
nations of the world, must not allow the world to actually
experience the Roman Empire scenario. I believe that the key
that will allow us to do this is management and innovation.

Simply stated, as you indicated in *Post-Capitalist Society*, by
applying intelligence to create innovation continually, and by
increasing intellectual productivity through management, it
is possible to convert all of the members of an organization
into social contributors, and to convert the organization into
a social entity with the objective of contributing to society. I

believe that these are the most effective and the only conceivable practical ways of protecting our advanced nations from falling and degenerating, and that they are the highest-priority items which executives have the responsibility to fulfill.

Corporations and nonprofit organizations

If we follow this point to its logical end, corporations must come closer and closer to nonprofit organizations, with the sole objective of being social entities or social contributors. The significance of the existence of corporations which do not have nonprofit organization-type concepts must, in the future, decrease at a dramatic pace. However, in Japan, the concept of the nonprofit organization has not been established yet, and it is not clear what model should be used in the establishment of this concept. In particular, purely private-sector nonprofit organizations in Japan have not made it past the development stage.

In your many publications, you have stated your ideas on these topics numerous times. I fully understand that it is extremely tedious for you to have to explain once again the importance of innovation to prevent the degeneration of society. However, I believe that it is of real significance for Japanese executives who, despite their usual excellence, are suffering from the recession and tend to become backward-looking, and for young people who must look to the future and steadily prepare for reform, to be exposed to a vision of the future while being aware of *The Future Which Has Already Happened*. With that in mind, as a method of preventing the world from making the mistakes of Rome, I must ask you for your opinion, from the perspective of innovation and management, on what corporations can learn from nonprofit organizations.

January 9, 1995

There is need for a social sector to rebuild community
Peter Drucker

Collapse of the Roman Empire

Dear Mr Nakauchi: You asked what societies can and must do to avoid the fate of Imperial Rome, in which society disintegrated to the point that the Barbarians could take over without encountering resistance.

What caused the internal collapse and disintegration of Roman society? This is an old question, first raised many centuries ago. It has occupied some of the West's best thinkers. It is indeed a puzzling question. For 250 or 300 years, from the time of Augustus in the first century after Christ until well into the fourth century, the Roman Empire was probably the stablest and most peaceful political system the world has ever seen. In fact, many historians believe that there was probably no other time in human history where there was such a long period of peace, prosperity and safety (though the people who are saying this seem never to have heard of Tokugawa Japan). Only a century before the Barbarians overran the Empire, Roman society revitalized itself in spectacular fashion when it embraced Christianity. Up to the very moment the Barbarians arrived, Rome had a very productive intellectual life; it was in the first decade of the fifth century that the foundations of western civilization were laid by the philosophers and theologians who fused the Greek heritage of classical antiquity, and especially of Plato, with Christian spirituality. Yet, when the Barbarians overran the military defenses of the Empire, the population in most parts actually welcomed them, or at least acquiesced. There have been many attempts to explain this, with each historian coming up with a different explanation. None, however, is fully convincing and fully persuasive.

Collapse of the Chinese civilization

It is not just the Roman Empire that raises the question of the decay of civilizations. The Chinese Empire, in the last two centuries, was similarly unable to resist corrosion and to maintain its society and its civilization against the pressures of new ideas, new technologies and new economic challenges. Surely the Chinese civilization ranks as high as the civilization of Greek and Roman antiquity ever did. Viewed from the outside, there were no signs that anything was seriously amiss.

The Qing Dynasty was no different from any of its predecessors. The arts flourished to the very end – in fact, a good deal of Qing Dynasty painting shows Chinese art at its very best. And yet, at the first challenge, around two hundred years ago, Chinese society proved itself to be totally hollow. Mao re-established political unity, but he did so by force and from above. It is very doubtful indeed, I would say, whether Chinese society has regained its cohesion, its strength, or its vitality. The moment political coercion relaxes even the least little bit, Chinese society seems to be in total disarray and as incapable of recreating a modern, and yet Chinese society, as it was a hundred years ago.

Collapse of the Ottoman Empire

The same was true of the Ottoman Empire. In its glory days, around 1600, it had as vibrant a society and civilization as anything Rome or China had. Yet, a century later, when confronted with new challenges, especially with the challenge of the ideas of modern Europe as it emerged after Renaissance and Reformation, Ottoman society dissolved. For two hundred years military power could maintain the political cohesion of the Empire, as military power had maintained the political cohesion of the Roman Empire. But Ottoman society became dysfunctional very rapidly, and never revitalized itself.

The philosophy of Arnold Toynbee

The conclusion philosophers of history have drawn from this – most notable in recent times are the nineteenth century Swiss, Jakob Burckhardt, and the twentieth century Englishman, Arnold Toynbee – is that there is a 'natural' life-cycle of civilizations and societies which is as incapable of being reversed or even of being arrested as is age in the human being.

If one accepts this philosophy, there is little point in asking what society can do to revitalize itself. Then the proper question is: 'At what stage of society's life-cycle are we now?' The answer to that question would probably not be a very optimistic one. There is no doubt that societies in the developed world are under severe stress and pressure. In many ways, perhaps information is to our present-day society what the Barbarians were to Imperial Rome, or the West to Imperial China. It dissolves existing traditional communities, those of family and small town and kinship.

The lesson of the Meiji era

There is one important exception to what an American philosopher, Brooks Adams, early in this century called the 'Law of Civilization and Decay.' It is the Meiji era of Japan. There, an old society threatened by internal decomposition and external aggression successfully revitalized itself. I hope you will allow me to suggest that the answer to your question, 'How can a society revitalize itself?' has to begin with an attempt to explain what happened at Meiji.

I have been asking this question for sixty years – ever since, in 1934, still very young and working at a London bank I first (and purely by accident) encountered Japanese art. I am handicapped by the fact that I cannot read Japanese and must depend on translations, but insofar as I can tell, there is little awareness, either in Japan or in the West, of the uniqueness of the Japanese experience and of its importance. Japanese historians do not seem to be aware of the fact that Meiji is the one exception in recorded history. Until very recently, the West paid little attention to Japan – and still, by and large, knows very little about your country. Thus the explanation I have come to accept is my own, and cannot claim to rest on thorough historical knowledge and study.

Meiji already established by Bunjin

However, it seems to me to be a convincing one: the Bunjin, a hundred years earlier, had already created the new Japan. Western ideas, Western technology, and Western institutions then simply became tools to realize the profoundly new, but also profoundly Japanese civilization and society which the Bunjin of the Kyoto Renaissance (it reached its peak I would say, between 1770 and 1810), had already established in their own lives, in their own work, and in their own values and beliefs. For a hundred years Bunjin culture was a private culture rather than the official one. But when the official culture collapsed – and it collapsed as much because of its own internal decay as because of the pressures from the outside – the Bunjin culture was ready to take over and to create the new Japan.

Obviously, it would require many pages for me to explain what I mean – far more than we have space for, and for beyond my knowledge. But here are a few examples of what I mean.

Education by Bunjin

Where Tokugawa society was rigidly stratified and, at least in theory, rejected any social mobility, the Bunjin knew no class lines. They were a perfect meritocracy, with the standing of the individual totally dependent on his learning and his achievement as an artist, a writer, or a historian. Where Tokugawa adhered to the Chinese idea that education was the privilege of the 'gentleman,' the Bunjin believed in universal literacy. By the early years of the nineteenth century, they had established schools, open to all youngsters of ability, in the domain of every Daimyo. By the time Meiji came around, Japan, as a result, had become the world's most literate country, way ahead of the literacy of any European country of that time. Meiji, thus, could immediately draw upon an educated, or at least a literate population, otherwise, Meiji could not have succeeded. It is surely no accident that every single one of the great men of Meiji had been the student of one of the prominent Bunjin scholars or of someone trained by one of the great Bunjin scholars. It is also clearly the legacy of the Bunjin that Japan (alone but for the US) has distinguished private universities founded by individuals (for example, Keio, Waseda and Hitotsubashi – now a government university, but founded as a private institution). This legacy also enabled Meiji Japan to produce educated leaders in all areas, in government, the judiciary; medicine, technology, and business – whereas both China until recently and India, well into this century, had to rely almost totally on Westerners to do jobs that required modern knowledge.

Bunjin as a 'social sector'

The reason why I stress this is that the Bunjin were not officials. On the contrary, when they first began their work they were viewed with suspicion and, indeed, with hostility by the Tokugawa Establishment, with many of the early Bunjin leaders actually being persecuted for their lack of orthodoxy. The Bunjin circles of scholars, writers and artists were what we would today call 'nonprofits.' The Bunjin schools were for a long time totally private. By and large the Bunjin were completely apolitical – to be anything else in late Edo would have been suicide, considering the pervasiveness of the Tokugawa police. They were outside of anything governmental or anything official. They were a 'social sector,' rather than a 'public sector.'

As I said, Japan is the one exception to the so-called 'Law of Civilization and Decay.' And the one thing that is unique and distinct in late Edo Japan is the Bunjin, that is, the 'nonprofit social sector' which they created. Most of the discussions of the Bunjin I have read discuss them as artists, for example, as painters or calligraphers. But the Bunjin movement was a genuine Renaissance and embraced an enormous range of knowledge and disciplines – mathematics, history, especially Japanese history, philosophy, medicine and so on. In other words, the values which the Bunjin created and represented permeated Japanese society and in fact became Japanese society. These values became the values on which Meiji could build and which enabled Meiji to use Western institutions and practices as tools to revitalize Japanese society.

Rebuilding the community

The lesson, at least to me, of the Meiji story is that to revitalize society there is a need for a social sector which rebuilds the community, and does so on the basis of individual performance and of concern for the community, that is, on the basis of values. And this sector has to be non-governmental.

January 12, 1995

Through volunteer work in the social sector, one can regain citizenship
Peter Drucker

WHAT GOVERNMENT CAN do well will, as discussed in the next part of this dialogue, become one of the central questions in politics, government, and political science during the next decade. It is highly controversial. And the evidence is by no means unambiguous.

What government cannot do

There is very little doubt about one thing that government cannot do. Government is not good at social tasks, the tasks of the community. Yet, this is what all Western governments have been trying to do since World War II – and usually with disastrous results.

Of all the governments of developed countries, only Japan has largely resisted the temptation for government to become the undertaker of social and community tasks. This in large measure explains, I would submit, why Japan alone of all developed countries still has considerable respect for government, and why government in Japan still has considerable effectiveness – much more so than government in any Western country.

Government resources will certainly remain a main source of finance for the tasks of society. Actually, government's role in financing social tasks may increase. Government will also remain charged with the task of setting standards for social sector performance, especially where government pays the bill. But in all developed countries – and especially in the developed countries of the West – there is growing disenchantment with government as the actual doer and performer of community tasks. Only thirty years ago – the high point was probably the Kennedy administration in the US – it was widely believed that government could and should do whatever community tasks might be required. Now, only thirty years later, powerful groups enjoying broad popular support (for example, the Republicans who won the 1994 Congressional election in the US) are convinced that there is no social task which government should actually do itself.

But there are social problems. There are community tasks. And in a period of major transition such as the one we are living through, those problems and tasks are increasing both in number and in seriousness. There is need therefore, for a social sector that is non-governmental.

The role of business

I said 'non-governmental' and not 'nonprofit.' For, to a very substantial extent, it is business that is uniquely qualified to satisfy social and community needs.

The best example I know is how business solved a central social problem of post-World War II Japan: the conflict between the social need to maintain the small and marginal retailer - the 'Mom & Pop stores' – with the economic need for efficient distribution. When I first came to Japan forty years ago, everyone already knew that Japanese distribution was woefully backward and totally unsuited to a modern economy, apart from being exceedingly expensive. Yet the small Mom & Pop stores served what was then an absolutely essential social function. It was the 'social safety-net' of Japanese society. This – not always with full justification – was usually given as the explanation why Japan needed a distribution system that saddled the country and the country's consumers with exorbitant prices. And then the new distributors converted the social problem of the Mom & Pop stores into a profitable business opportunity by turning Mom & Pop stores into franchises. This maintained their social function and, at the same time, provided as efficient a distribution system as any country in the world now has.

To convert social problems and social challenges into profitable business opportunities is the ideal solution for the problems of the social sector.

The role of the social sector

However, this solution is not always possible. For the majority of social and community problems, we need special institutions, the ones I call the institutions of the 'social sector.' Normally, they are called 'nonprofits.' It is usually believed that they represent 'charity.' Increasingly, however, these institutions are not being financed by charity, that is, by voluntary donations. They are, instead, financed as contractors to governments, or they are financed by charging fees.

One example of social sector institutions being financed as government contractors is the voucher system, which is now being proposed as a solution to the poor performance of the

American public school. Under a voucher system, parents who are not satisfied with the performance of the public school in their neighborhood can put their child into a private school; the 'voucher' pays the private school the equivalent of what the child would cost the State in a public school. Another example is the way American and Japanese largely private hospitals are being paid out of the tax money of their country's health-care insurance systems.

Increasingly, too, social sector institutions are being paid out of fees rather than out of donations. One example is the way the private universities in Japan manage to finance themselves primarily out of the fees they charge for entrance examinations and admissions.

But 'nonprofit' is also a misnomer. It makes very little difference, in fact, whether these institutions are legally run for profit, or legally run for non profit.

A good many American hospitals, especially the large ones, have in the last thirty years become for-profit companies. But it makes absolutely no difference to the patients, to the physicians who work at the hospital, or to the hospital staff; whether the hospital is legally run for profit or not, it operates in exactly the same way.

The purpose of institutions of the social sector

What characterizes these so-called nonprofit institutions of the social sector is their purpose. A government demands compliance. A business sells goods or services. The social sector institutions aim at changing a human being. The purpose of the hospital is not a 'satisfied customer.' It is a cured patient. The purpose of the school is not a 'satisfied customer'. It is a student who has learned enough to become a different person and to lead a different life and career. Various health research associations in the US – the American Heart Association, for instance, or the American Cancer Society – have for their purpose the prevention or cure of fatal human diseases. They have played a leading role in the medical advances of the last fifty years. Community organizations such as the Girl Scouts or Boy Scouts aim at instilling into young people self-discipline, standards, self-respect, purpose, and skills. The purpose of the oldest of our community institutions, the religious organizations such as the churches, is not even limited to this world. It is to produce a human being whose life and whose afterlife have been profoundly changed.

Management

Because the purpose of the social sector institutions is to change human beings and to change human society, government is incapable of doing these tasks well. But for this reason, these tasks also elude business. They require institutions which have different values and different goals. These institutions require management fully as much as business or a government agency. In fact, they require better management since, unlike a business, they do not have the discipline of a financial bottom line. But they also require very different management.

Restoration of citizenship

These institutions in today's developed countries serve a second and equally important purpose: they restore community and with it, effective citizenship.

Within the last hundred years, but especially in the last fifty years, traditional communities everywhere have been dissolved. At the beginning of this century, most people, even in the most highly developed country, lived in traditional communities such as a village. The family was then still the only effective social agent. Even if people today still live in a rural surrounding, they do not live in a 'village.' Information and communications have made every village a part of the world. Even in the smallest village people today identify themselves far more with their work and their profession than they do with the local community.

Change of families

Precisely because the family is no longer a survival necessity, as it was only a hundred short years ago, it is no longer the dominant community for most of us. At its best, it provides love, affection and happiness. At its very worst, it is a burden. My grandmother, to cite only one example, knew where every one of her second and third cousins was, and what he or she was doing – and there were some thirty of them. I barely know my own first cousins, and do not know their children at all. They live much too far away.

Change of village and town

For ours is a world in which fewer and fewer people finish their lives in the town – let alone in the house – in which they were born (as my great grandmother still did when she died in 1920, aged almost one hundred). Traditional communities no longer provide the central bond for today's educated people. But people do need a community.

New community

In the US this is being provided more and more frequently by work as a volunteer in a social sector organization. Unlike the traditional communities, the social sector organization provides a voluntary community – one can join and one can also leave. It provides a genuine community.

One example – in many ways the best one I can think of – are the fast-growing pastoral Christian churches in the US. A growing problem in developed societies is the gulf between highly educated young people, who have gone to university and now hold responsible positions as knowledge workers, and their parents, who are typically farmers or blue-collar workers. The two love each other, but they do not share experience, problems, or interests. And here the church provides a new community for them which brings them together, not only in common worship but in common work as volunteers either in the work of the church itself (for example, running the youth group or the church music), or in the church's work in the community (working with alcoholics or drug addicts).

Meaning of citizenship

And then there is the growing need in modern society to provide an effective sphere of citizenship in which the individual can actually make decisions in and for the community. Citizenship is not, it should be stressed, a legal term. It originally meant to be a member of the city, that is, a responsible and active member of a community. This is no longer possible in the complex nation-state, even the fairly small one such as, for example, Switzerland. Citizenship in the body politics increasingly means only two things: to vote once in a while, and to pay taxes all the time. That is not enough, however, to maintain a democracy. This explains the increasing alienation of the individual from political society.

What can the community do for me?

It leads increasingly to an attitude where the question is not, 'What can I do for the community?' but 'What can the community do for me?' It leads to dependence on the state – and this, as Mr Nakauchi's question implies, was of course a major reason why Rome collapsed. All free inhabitants of the Roman Empire had Roman citizenship. And yet their citizenship had become meaningless. They had increasingly come to see the Empire only as a source of free food and benefits, rather than as a community to which they could make a contribution, and in which they made a difference. In the end they no longer cared whether their governors were fellow-Romans or German Barbarians.

In the social sector organizations, volunteers are again citizens. They increasingly run the organization – as they do, for instance, in the fast-growing pastoral churches in the US. There the clergy are not the 'bosses' but members of the community who do a special job, with the other tasks being done primarily by volunteers. The same is increasingly true of community organizations such as the Girl Scouts and Boy Scouts.

Meaning of citizenship

In the US we have reached the point where every other adult – some ninety million people – works for three to five hours a week as a volunteer. It is not the retired people who are the core volunteers. Highly educated, affluent, knowledgeable workers aged between thirty five and forty five – and especially couples in which both husband and wife work – provide the volunteer work force for the social sector. Whenever such people are asked why they do this work, when they are already busy enough in their job and in taking care of their children, they give the same answer: 'Because in my volunteer work in the social sector, I make a difference. I am a citizen.'

What business can learn

This, by the way, is a major reason why business can learn a good deal from social sector organizations. Increasingly, the key employees in business will be highly educated, knowledgeable people. Knowledgeable people have mobility even in countries in which it is considered normal for people to stay with one employer – that means, primarily, in Japan of course. And they know it. To attract them, and to hold them, a business must look upon them as 'volunteers.' It must look upon them as people who must want to stay and must want to contribute – or else they will drift away sooner or later.

Managing knowledge workers as volunteers

Knowledge workers therefore have to be managed as if they were volunteers. Volunteers in nonprofit institutions are, of course, not paid. They therefore do not have the satisfaction of a paycheck. By and large, there are no promotions in nonprofit institutions, either – there is only a progression to work that makes greater demands and imposes greater responsibilities. The nonprofit institutions of the social sector, therefore, have to give volunteers much greater satisfaction than a business has to do. What then can we learn from the successful nonprofit institutions about managing knowledge workers?

The first thing we have to learn is that volunteers in a nonprofit institution – and this is true the world over – demand a clear and focused mission. They demand to know what the institution they serve is trying to achieve. Increasingly, they also demand of the institutions accountability for results. They also demand responsibility in their own volunteer work. And increasingly they demand training.

In the US (but increasingly in Europe as well) volunteers also demand that their performance be appraised.

But at the same time, they expect that they will have a major say in the management of the organization. They demand at least substantial participation. Business will have to learn all these things to manage knowledge workers successfully.

Historical background

Social sector institutions are most advanced in the US. The main reason is historical: religious organizations in America, such as churches, have not been supported by the tax payer as they have been all over Europe. They had to raise their own money. Since money was, therefore, very scarce, they had to mobilize volunteers from the community to do most of the work. In Europe every country – even the smallest – tried to impose religious conformity on its subjects. There was thus no competition between religious denominations within a territory. But in the US there was religious pluralism from the earliest days of settlement on this continent. This meant that every religious denomination had to develop the ability to hold and attract community and volunteer support.

Fifty years ago, I thought that business enterprise would become the new community in industrial society. Europe during the late 1920s and early 1930s had convinced me of the collapse of social cohesion and community that underlay the rise of totalitarianism, both Nazism and Stalinism (as I explained in my first book *The End of Economic Man* which appeared in 1938-39). In fact, I became interested in management not because I was interested in business – at that time I knew nothing of business.

Community in business enterprises

I became interested in management around 1940 (just before the US went to war), because I saw in the big business enterprise the new integrating social agency. This is the reason why I advocated employment security, a guaranteed annual wage, and a self-governing community in charge of the social aspects of life and work in the industrial factory (especially in my book, *The Future of Industrial Man*, which originally appeared in 1943 in the middle of World War II).

In the West these ideas never found much resonance. But – totally independent of anything I had written – Japan moved very far in the direction to which I had pointed. In retrospect, it is supreme irony that employment stability was imposed during World War II by the Japanese military in order to prevent workers from leaving jobs, and against strenuous opposition by the workers. Employment stability and lifetime employment, after World War II, became the social covenant on which Japan based her recovery and her economic growth. For that reason alone, I hope that Japan (even in the radical industrial transformation we are now going through) will maintain the basic commitment to the mutuality of obligations between employer and employee, and to the employing organization as being a community of interest for all those who work there.

New organization

Even so, it is quite clear that the industrial community cannot do what I hoped it would do fifty years ago. For knowledge people – increasingly the determining and largest group in the work force – the employing organization cannot take the place of family and community. For many years to come, I expect, the employing organization in Japan will mean more to the individual knowledge worker than it has come to mean in the West. For in the US and increasingly in Europe, the knowledge worker has come to see in the employing organization only a means of accomplishing his own ends. Increasingly in the West the employing organization will therefore have to learn to motivate the knowledge worker to focus on the ends and values of the organization rather than to subordinate those to this own ends and his own gods. The same trend is certainly going to be effective in Japan, as well – it is inherent in the nature of knowledge. Thus, in Japan, too, the need for the core of the new work force, that is, for highly educated knowledge people, to have a meaningful community of their own, and a community they can freely choose, will become important. And that need can only be met by social sector organizations.

What this means for Japan

Japan, too – like the US – had religious pluralism, with the various sects each in need of building community support, but also providing community services. Meiji converted the religious groups, both Buddhist and Shinto, into organs of the state on the European model; then the community-service tradition disappeared in Japan. But both the roots and the need are there. A Japanese social sector will surely look very different from an American social sector, and both will look very different from the social sector of any European country. The social sector, far more than government or business, represents the traditional values of a culture. It represents the traditions and values of the local community. But yet one can, I think, anticipate with reasonable certainty that within the next twenty or thirty years Japan will develop a vigorous social sector of her own.

But above all, Japan provides one example of revitalizing a society – the example of the Bunjin who regenerated an ossified and stagnant Tokugawa society, and thus laid the foundations for the one successful modernization of a non-Western culture, the Meiji achievement.

January 12, 1995

Each of us must endeavour to influence and change our society based on the principles of self-offering, self-discipline and self-responsibility
Isao Nakauchi

Self-offering, self-discipline and self-responsibility

When I think of Western history, Professor Drucker, I always lament the absence of the concept of citizenship in Japan. The Western countries have made the transition from feudal societies to nation states through the process of revolution. Through their own efforts, and sometimes by sacrificing their lives, the people gained their freedom and became true citizens. The men and women of those times recognized the need to accept responsibility for addressing problems within the organizations to which they belonged in order to obtain freedom and citizenship. Thus, the citizens of the West have held the principles of self-offering, self-discipline and self-responsibility to be their own in an inalienable sense.

In contrast, Japan has had little experience as a nation state since it moved directly from a feudal society to a monolithic state. With few exceptions, the people have had little time in which to develop the concept of citizenship. The concept of freedom itself was introduced to the Japanese by the Americans after World War II. Consequently, many Japanese believe (and this is often borne out in postwar policy) that freedom is something guaranteed by and dispensed by an absolute authority, rather than something to be gained through one's own efforts. Freedom is understood to be something approved by one's superiors; there is no perception that freedom carries with it the duty to act with self-offering, self-discipline and self-responsibility as a citizen of the state. So the Japanese people, as free citizens, call for freedom, but when something goes wrong, they forget self-responsibility and instead seek protection from the government. This is seen as the natural right of the citizens. A long-running campaign on administrative reform has finally brought home the importance of deregulation and structural reform to the Japanese people; yet when I talk of the need for administrative reform or deregulation, our company becomes subject to protest campaigns by various industries and groups using protest letters, telephone calls, demonstrations and leaflets. Each

151

time, it is sad to note that the protesters did not appreciate that deregulation for the benefit of society as a whole must come before their own interests.

Change by wisdom

As you point out, the limitations of government are already plain to all. Government cannot claim to be able to reign over the people as the leader of the people's society. This applies to all leading industrialized nations, and Japan is no exception. The government here no longer has the capacity to act as leader of the people's society. Now, more than ever, is the time for every Japanese to assert himself or herself as a citizen.

We need not ammunition but wisdom. As many of us as possible must use our wisdom to influence and change the economy and society. When structural change is overdue, when the Japanese economy and society fail to anticipate changing times and world trends, then we will become the weaker party left by the wayside, the streets will be overflowing with the ranks of the unemployed, society will degenerate and the country will go to ruin. A look at the world around us shows that there is an economic limit to the revenue of a country. Governments are clearly no longer the leaders of society, unable to answer the needs of all with benevolence and generosity, and the people should wake up to this fact.

But this is only the first step. The world is already moving toward the post-capitalist society, and Japan must go with the flow. In fact, Japan has no choice but to go with the flow. To do this, we have to get rid of regulations that restrict economic activity, and develop an authentic free market economy in Japan. If we stay as we are now, refusing to address structural change because of fears of hollowing out, refusing to acknowledge the potential of international division of labor, accepting without reservation the cost of economic regulations, then the Japanese economy will be left behind as the global economy moves forward, and we will be isolated. A no-win situation like this would cause economic recession and social impoverishment, a heavy load to bear as the country begins to age on an unprecedented scale.

As you point out, however, the Japanese people are clever. We achieved the Meiji Restoration; we are not so complacent to simply lie down and let such a gloomy future overrun us. All of us must be prepared to see ourselves as citizens, endeavouring to influence and change our society through our own efforts to fulfill the needs of an advanced society, based on the principles of self-offering, self-discipline and self-responsibility. This surely constitutes the one and only way to revitalize society.

Seeds of change – dedication of volunteers

The seeds of this change are already in evidence in Japan; I have watched the process evolving before my eyes in the dedicated work of volunteers working to help victims of the recent earthquake. Some of these volunteers hired cars to bring water and packed lunches into the disaster area; others helped sort through relief supplies pouring in from around the country to the Hyogo prefectural offices and Kobe City Hall; still others served noodles and other hot meals to victims sheltering in parks and elsewhere in the cold. They came from all over the country, entirely of their own volition, to help in any way they could. Their dedication and sense of organization were both stunning to behold and on a level unprecedented for our country.

The word 'volunteer' is often associated with selflessness and virtue in Japan, where volunteer activity has only just started to take off and wide differences still exist in perceptions and capabilities in the field. Volunteer work was marred by deficiencies and duplications and was not always, it has to be said, entirely beneficial to the people and places it was designed to help.

But the real significance of recent volunteer efforts to relieve the suffering of earthquake victims lies not so much in the emerging concept of volunteer work as in the fact that many people actually went to the disaster zone and could acquire actual organizational and physical experience for themselves. Slowly but surely, this is changing the nature of both volunteer workers and wider society. For the Japanese people, selfless and organized efforts by citizens are indispensable to the continued vitality of society. It will still be some time, however, before we fully realize how the purpose of public sector institutions is to change people and society, as you pointed out in your letter. It is also necessary, I found, to acknowledge our responsibility to pave the ground for raising young citizens who are self-motivated and are eager to change society for the better.

As noted in *The Post-Capitalist Society*, it is the duty of executives and the role of management in industrialized countries to imbue employees with this sense of purpose, to turn people into contributors.

I shall never forget what I have learned through this experience. It has renewed my determination to succeed as an executive.

Information and the local community

With respect to corporate principles, I believe that Daiei can learn a great deal from Recruit, a pioneer in the Japanese information industry. Under a joint agreement with Recruit announced in May 1992, I assumed the office of Chairman. The media were very keen to know why I accepted shares in a company associated with a major scandal destined to earn a place in Japanese history. My response was that such agreements enable companies to carve out new areas of business. Recruit represented the most attractive partner in such an undertaking.

Recruit is a young company with a corporate spirit of freedom and magnanimity. Their corporate philosophy, rare in Japan, stresses the individual ability of each employee. Recruit employees have considerable leeway to demonstrate individual flair. Innovative ideas and proposals from younger employees are actively utilized. Employees are encouraged to build on their own ideas in identifying the information needs of consumers and developing the appropriate information services. Recruit is renowned for giving employees the freedom to develop their ideas and to express their potential.

In recognition of the importance of the community you describe, Recruit has recently brought out a local magazine called *Lifestyle Information 360°*. The magazine provides a wealth of detailed information on services in the local area. Like a knowledgeable friend in times of need, *Lifestyle Information 360°* provides its readers with answers to everyday but important queries such as the address of local night schools or the hours of local child-care centers.

You pointed out in your letter that there is a growing need in modern society to provide a sphere of citizenship in which the individual can actually make decisions in and for the community. The earthquake has proved that the importance of making a contribution to the community is rising in Japan, as elsewhere. The problem is the almost complete absence of media on the scene to inform us of what was required and how to contribute. We were given an overload of information; yet most of the information came from Tokyo. With the exception of Tokyo, the Japanese people have virtually no detailed information about their own locality. Recruit is one company working to make up for this weakness in the Japanese-style information society. It regards the contribution of information services to the community as a social responsibility of the company, and is working to create success in this area ahead of its competitors. Although this undertaking has just begun, Recruit is confident that there is an opportunity to explore a new business frontier.

Daiei and Recruit

I firmly believe that Recruit can carve out a future for itself in Japan and indeed the world. With its unique approach and a good appreciation of social and economic changes in Japan, Recruit will be able to utilize information to generate innovative solutions from the opportunities provided by change. This is possible precisely because Recruit employees, like NPO members, see change in people, society and themselves through information and knowledge as a perfectly natural process. Like young leaders of developing countries, the 'executives of tomorrow' are receiving a thorough grounding from this rare type of company.

I view Recruit as a prime example of the information-linked flat organization of which you speak. In this sense, Daiei has much to learn from the organizational and management philosophy at Recruit, which emphasizes a progressive spirit and the importance of using the opportunities provided by major economic and social change to develop new services accurately tailored to the needs of consumers. As well as learning from Recruit, Daiei will be working on a joint venture with the company in developing new areas of business to revitalize the flagging Japanese economy. In this, we will make effective use of the growing Daiei national network of stores and the Recruit information network, bearing in mind your words: 'Businesses stay in competition and both attain and maintain leadership by systematically looking for changes that have already occurred inside and outside, and asking , 'Is this an opportunity?'

February 25, 1995

9

Reinventing government

What are your views on government regulation and the role of government in a free market? What is your advice on reinventing government?

Isao Nakauchi

Reevaluation of government

Professor Drucker, your letter implies that, at a time when the world is undergoing massive change, private enterprises, workers, executives and the general public of industrialized countries must be prepared to reject traditionally-held beliefs and notions and make their own efforts to better society and the economy. This is no doubt a daunting and difficult prospect for some. It is also a highly challenging task. We, the executives of Japan, must tackle the challenge with courage and sagacity, rather than useless pessimism about the future.

I believe that this applies equally to the public sector. Governments must reevaluate their work and form structures that can adapt to tumultuous changes in economy and society. Below I have set out four questions about reinventing government.

Free market economy

My first question is about the free market economy.

The Japanese economy has been described as a planned economy posing as a capitalist economy. This can be attributed to the widespread perception, both at home and abroad, that government industrial policy, based on production priorities, was responsible for the spectacularly successful economic growth that occurred after the war. While I would not refute this claim, I believe that other factors were also at work. The Japanese economy rose to life like a phoenix from the ashes of the war, to use your words, because the US and the rest of the world opened their markets to us, and because Japan itself joined the countries of market economies. I would be grateful for your opinion on how free market principles should operate in Japan, and for your views on the significance and relevance of the free market economy. Those will serve as guidelines for Japanese executives.

Regulation and the task of government

My second question is about the purpose of regulation, and my third, related question is about the role of government.

The Japanese government is now at the point where it is required to rethink its approach to economic policy and the true role of government itself.

I believe that with respect to economic affairs, the role of government should be confined to providing a minimum set of rules designed to preserve the structure of society: the Anti-Monopoly Law, the Product Liability Law, the Administrative Procedures Law, the Basic Law on the Environment and so on. Such legislation should of course be reviewed continually to keep pace with change. And I believe (and I am not alone here) that government should ideally be as small as possible. It must leave daily economic affairs to free market principles.

Many politicians like to argue publicly the need for small government, as do top-level bureaucrats and the media. In this sense, small government is already approaching the status of national policy. This objective, then, should be part of the government policies being produced.

Unfortunately, there is no evidence of any such efforts in the policies currently being practised. The government is not interested in examining what it can achieve.

Thus, government must look closely at the issue you raised in *The New Realities*, namely, not what should be done but what it can achieve. Then it must clarify those tasks of which it is capable, sort them into priority order and promptly put them into effect.

In this sense, what the Japanese government can achieve right now is to lay the groundwork to encourage a future private-sector-led resurgence in economic activity. This will also contribute to preparing for the uncertain future, in which we will soon see the arrival of the aging society.

I am calling for 'small government,' but I would certainly not say that government is unnecessary. In particular, for issues that require a global response, it is the responsibility of the governments of advanced countries to call on the international community to move in the direction of solving them. To achieve that most effectively, the governments of all countries must collectively combine their wisdom.

In *Post-Capitalist Society*, as an example of a sector in which there is a need for activities by international organizations on a global scale surpassing the nation state, you mentioned environmental issues and arms control. Even if we limit ourselves to just these two issues, evidently tremendous effort is required to move toward finding a solution: I think that this is true of all advanced countries without exception. In other words fiscal freedom is becoming smaller and there is a tendency for the burden to be placed upon the people and corporations.

Under such a situation, can the international community really solve global environmental issues? Furthermore, in the advanced countries, will there be a sufficient display of leadership toward the solution of these issues, either in terms of policy or in terms of capital?

I would very much like to hear your opinion on the issues for which the governments of the advanced countries must take a common approach, including the many issues that are facing the international community that has the potential to inflict mortal damage on all of humanity, and the proper modalities for nation states and international organization which you spoke in *Post-Capitalist Society*.

Reinventing of government

My fourth question concerns the reinventing of government itself.

159

In Japan, there are still those who ask whether the price of goods will fall if we alleviate and abolish price regulations and regulations on market entry. They ask whether taxes could be lowered by abolishing government-owned corporations that have lost the reason for their existence, and by eliminating subsidies for industries such as agriculture that have lost their international competitiveness. However, while those points certainly do merit debate, the true nature of the problem lies elsewhere. I think that we really should pay attention to whether we can transform the social structure, using administrative reforms as a tool. We would like your advice on the role of government.

Professor Drucker, the four questions in this letter are the last four questions I have. I would like to ask you about the correct modalities for government. I firmly believe that this is a problem common to all advanced countries around the world.

February 25, 1995

The great strength of the free market is that it minimizes threats and mistakes
Peter Drucker

Few people seem to realize that Communism and its planned economy collapsed, rather than that Democracy and the free market won. Communism and its planned economy collapsed because of their total failure: political, social, economic, moral and spiritual. They collapsed from within. Certainly they proved themselves vastly inferior to free government and free market. But this does not mean that free government and the free market have won. The best description is that they survived.

That means that there is no alternative to making both the free market and free government truly work. The opportunity to do so has been created by the total disappearance of what large masses in all countries considered true alternatives only a few years ago, but which are now totally discredited. But such an opportunity is, above all, a challenge. We will – rightly – demand a great deal more from free government and the free market, precisely because they are now the only players left on the world scene.

The free market cannot stand alone

There is a vocal though rather small group of people – the 'true believers' in free markets, such as the economists of the so-called 'Austrian' School – who believe that the free market, standing alone, creates an economy; that it creates a functioning society; and that it creates by itself a functioning government. But the evidence for this belief is not convincing. On the contrary, what is going on now in the former Soviet Union and in some of its Eastern European satellites such as Rumania and Bulgaria – but also in Mainland China – shows clearly that it is not enough to have a free market. There has to be a working social and political framework. There has to be a civil society. There has to be a legal structure. There have, above all, to be clear and legally guaranteed property rights. There has to be functioning and respected government. By itself a free market does not guarantee either a free or a functioning society and economy. Its absence, we now know, cripples society and the economy and, in the end, destroys both. Its presence is a necessary cause of both a

161

functioning society and economy, but, by itself, is not sufficient.

Necessary framework

This is the challenge which the free world, and especially the developed countries in it, now face. The true believers in a free market of the Austrian persuasion have shown convincingly that the market can organize far more than we believed over the last hundred years and especially during the last fifty years. Still, there are limits. There are clearly a great many basic relationships in society – and even in the economy – which market forces by themselves cannot handle. They are surely not able to organize the family, to organize a community, or to organize a nation. The very strength of the market is that its relationships are impersonal and free of any but economic value. But clearly, we are not ready to abolish regulations such as the one that says that only somebody with a degree from a recognized medical school is entitled to call himself a physician and to practice medicine. We are surely not willing to abolish the regulations that protect the public against charlatans, against fraud, or against gross incompetence in matters affecting the public good. We therefore need to think through both what the market can do and what it cannot – and should not be expected to – do.

Raison d'être of free market

What is the raison d'être, the reason for existence of the market, and the explanation of its superiority? One is that a modern economy is far too complex to be managed by any one agency or power. This is the central argument in what is probably the most persuasive of the pro-market theories of the last fifty years, the theory of the great Anglo-Austrian economist and social philosopher Friedrich von Hayek. No system can work that substitutes the judgment of any one person or any one agency for the reactions and decisions of untold numbers of small participants – firms and individuals – each acting on the information available to him or her. There is no way to obtain enough information, let alone to understand it. The market constitutes, so to speak, an infinite number of small, partially dependent computers, linked in parallel processing, each in possession of most (though probably not all) of the information needed to make a correct decision, precisely because it is a small and local decision. There is no way that a big mainframe computer – which is, in effect, what a planning bureaucracy tries to be – can possibly obtain the necessary information. But also, a planning bureaucracy must end up with the same decision for everything and everybody. To come out right, however, there has to be a variety of decisions, each slightly different, each responding to specific circumstances, each optimizing within a very narrow range of factors – for each of the local decision makers has a different situation, has different needs, wants and goals, and decides differently the question of the trade-off between cost and benefits.

Add to this – and it is an important addition – that there is no longer any one clear focus for the economic decision.

Realization by Ludwig Ehrhardt

For some decisions the focus is purely local, indeed purely individual. Central planning, except in a period of extreme scarcity in which necessities have to be rationed, simply ends with the same decision for all; this is the wrong decision for everyone. This is what the architect of Germany's economic recovery after World War II, Ludwig Ehrhardt, realized when he abolished rationing overnight, as soon as the worst of the post-War famine was over – and immediately triggered Germany's economic up-turn.

Other decisions have to be the right ones for a large area, whether a geographic area, a social class, or an economic group. Others may have to be right for a whole country. Now increasingly, the global economy is the focus in which real decisions have to be made - and for that there exists no planning bureaucracy. Also, there could not exist any planning bureaucracy for the simple reason that the information needed for decisions in the world economy does not exist and will never exist.

Mistakes are catastrophic in a planned economy

The raison d'être of the market, in other words, is not that it works well. The raison d'être is that nothing else can work at all. This has been amply proved over the last fifty years. The market works precisely because its mistakes are localized. Mistakes in a planned economy such as the Russians had - and such as the Chinese in part still try to maintain - are by definition enormous mistakes. In a planned economy, small mistakes are impossible, by definition. All mistakes are catastrophes.

Personal responsibility in free market

In the market there is personal responsibility. This means that a mistake is localized, but also that it is corrected locally. If an individual businessman makes a poor investment decision, his small business does not grow, but nothing else is hurt. Within any market even the largest corporation is a small individual. The biggest employer in any free market economy does not for instance employ more than one percent of the working population.

In the main car-producing countries, that is, in the US, in Japan, in Germany, in Italy, the automobile industry used to be the largest single manufacturing employer. The American automobile industry made horrendous mistakes in the 1980s. As a result, employment was slashed drastically, but the US economy barely felt any impact. There was suffering in two or three cities that depended primarily on automobile employment, such as Flint, outside Detroit. But fifty kilometers from Flint, those troubles were not even noticed. Because in a free market the individual decision-maker is personally responsible, mistakes are not catastrophic and become self-correcting.

Minimization of mistakes

This does not mean that the market is perfect. It does not mean that the market alone is enough. It only means, to emphasize it again, that there is no better mechanism around – and probably no better mechanism imaginable. The greatest strength of the market is not perhaps even that it optimizes opportunities (though it does). Its greatest strength is that it minimizes threats and mistakes.

Legal assurance of property rights

To repeat, the market presupposes a social framework. It also presupposes an effective government, and (as is being proven now by a great deal of historical research,) a functioning market requires respect for, and legal assurance of property rights. After long years of Totalitarian Communism there is little respect left for property rights, and no legal system to protect them. To restore the protection of property rights may be the most essential factor in enabling the former Communist world to build a solid, modern economy. The absence of property rights is the one thing that disturbs me most about Mainland China.

March 10, 1995

We need to avoid regulations that are not enforceable, that have outlived their usefulness and that penalize economic activity
Peter Drucker

The meaning of regulations

What then is the function of governmental regulations in a Free Market economy? Do they have any function at all?

Obviously, this is a very big subject - and far too big for this dialogue. I think Mr Nakauchi and I are in agreement that there are areas in which government regulation is needed. There is need for law - civil and criminal. There is unlikely to be much argument about the need for regulations which lay down standards for socially critical activities, such as regulations as to what credentials a school teacher or a physician has to have. There is surely not going to be much argument about the need for regulations that forbid adulteration of food or for regulations that forbid the discharge of pollutants into public waterways.

Globalized economy

But the question is not a generic one. The question is always whether this or that particular regulation is needed and in what form. And perhaps it might be a good idea in this age of the world economy to be a little more careful in issuing regulations than we have been in the past. We have learned in the US and in Japan that we need to consider in advance the environmental impact of any action of a government agency or of a business. We no longer take for granted – as did our grandparents – that the actions of human beings have no impact on the natural environment in which we live. Similarly, we need to learn that every government action needs to be reviewed as to its impact on the competitive position of a country or an industry in the world economy. We can no longer – as most bureaucracies still believe – maintain that there are purely 'domestic' regulations. We need an economic competitiveness statement for every proposed governmental legislation and governmental regulation. At least we need to know what price in terms of economic competitiveness we will have to pay for this or that domestic policy.

Japan's cost of living and competitiveness

Let me give you one example. When it was introduced, more than forty years ago, the Rice Subsidy was probably an absolute necessity for Japan. Few people, around 1950, thought it even remotely possible that Japan would ever be able to export enough manufactured goods to pay for large food imports. Now, however, all the Rice Subsidy does is to create a Japanese market for imports (mainly from the US) of wheat, corn, soybeans, chicken feed, meats, vegetables and oats. Without the Rice Subsidy, which pays every farmer to grow nothing else, Japan could probably grow the bulk of the food it imports – both soil and climate are good enough. As a result of the Rice Subsidy, however, Japan has become the one developed country most dependent on food imports, rather than the one least dependent on them, which is what the Rice Subsidy was intended to guarantee. It also has the highest food costs of any developed country, and with them the highest cost of living. The Japanese people might, of course, still prefer the Rice Subsidy despite its enormous cost in competitiveness. But a competitive-impact statement would at least acquaint them with the real economic costs of the subsidy.

Companies fleeing California

Competitive-impact statements might have prevented the severe economic crisis that now affects the State of California in the US. Twenty years ago California was the first choice for any business looking for a location in the US. In the last five years, however, businesses in increasing numbers, American businesses as well as foreign ones, are fleeing California. The main cause is a proliferation of regulations on the part of the State of California and of its cities. One example: even the slightest change to an existing building in California may require up to thirty different permits from more than a dozen state and local-government agencies. In the neighboring states of Arizona and Nevada, the same change usually requires only one permit. As a result, it sometimes takes four years in California to get permission to add to a building. In Arizona or Nevada it takes three days. The three states have identical building codes - the differences are all in the proliferation of rules and regulatory agencies in California over the last twenty years.

It would not have happened had the State and its agencies had to think through and publish a competitive-impact statement before imposing these rules.

Burden and benefit of regulations

Regulations are a burden on the economy. In many cases the burden is greatly overbalanced by the benefits. The burden of meat inspection is surely greatly outbalanced by the benefit of eliminating - or at least limiting - wholesale food poisoning, as might otherwise occur. But we need to know the tradeoffs. In a competitive World Economy, burdens can no longer be seen as being purely local.

A great many regulations impose only burdens and confer no benefits. They were either always deleterious, or they have become so.

Regulations that are unenforceable

The first category are regulations that are unenforceable. The biggest example in this century was the American attempt to enforce the prohibition of alcoholic beverages in the 1920s. All it did was to create gangsters. Today governments all over the world are trying to impose local regulations on the World Economy, and especially on the movement of information and money. They are simply unenforceable.

Control of transnational money flow

Maybe we will, within the next few decades, create transnational public agencies that can control the transnational flows of money. By now they exceed the transnational flow of goods. In 1993 – the last year for which we have figures – transnational investment flows amounted to at least five trillion US dollars, whereas flows of goods and services came to only four trillion US dollars. No central bank can possibly regulate these investment flows – even though all of them desperately try. In fact, even if the major central banks – those of the US, Japan, the UK, Germany, and France – work together, as they did in the dollar crisis a few months back, the results are just plain laughable. So were the results of the desperate efforts of major central banks around last Christmas to prevent the collapse of the Mexican Peso. A strong argument can be made that we need a World Central Bank as badly as the nineteenth century needed National Central Banks – the argument that in the end led to the English Central Bank Act which, by 1914, had been copied by every single country in the world including, of course, Japan. So far, we have no such instrument, and we do not know how to design it, let alone how to run it, and govern it. So the smart thing is not to try to regulate. Unenforceable regulations, as the example of America's Prohibition shows, can only do harm.

Regulations that have become useless

Another category of regulations that are deleterious are regulations that have outlived their usefulness. One of the great political inventions of the nineteenth century was an American one: the regulation of so-called 'natural monopolies.' Industries which by their nature were monopolies – the railroads in America, for instance, which in the late nineteenth century enjoyed what seemed an unbreakable monopoly on land transportation – had, so the argument went, to be regulated lest they abuse their monopoly power. Outside the US, such industries were nationalized: The railroads, the telephone, the telegraph, electric power. In the US, alone in the developed world, they remained in private hands but under strict regulation. For a century this worked well. But by now every one of these industries has been deprived by new technology of its monopoly power. At this point, continued regulation becomes counter-productive. It can only do damage – and just as much to the former monopoly industry as to society and the economy. Then deregulation is needed.

Regulation of the airlines

In some cases the need is for open competition – which is the way we in the US are going in respect to telecommunications. In other industries, however, new but different regulation is needed.

One example is air traffic. In the air there are only so many airways in which planes can safely fly at the same time. Since an airplane cannot stop in mid-air, air lanes have to be controlled. Competition in air traffic – in respect to fares, for instance, and to services offered passengers – can be unrestricted. The American example is most instructive in that deregulation of the airlines has produced a number of efficient, safe, and cheap competitors such as SouthWest Airlines, which despite – or perhaps because of – its low fares is the most profitable American airline today. But the number of planes at any given time in any given airway, and with it the number of carriers that can be permitted to fly from one point to another, has to be regulated simply because in the air there is no such thing as unlimited space. Each airway constitutes, in traditional terms, a 'natural monopoly.'

Meaningless separation of banking from investment banking

Regulations, no matter how badly needed at any one time, and how beneficial at that time, always become obsolete eventually.

Sixty years ago, in the midst of the Great Depression, it seemed perfectly logical and indeed necessary in the US to separate commercial banking business from investment banking business. By now, the separation has become meaningless. All it does now is to shift financial business in America increasingly from the traditional banks to non-banks which are under no such restrictions. Also, an obsolete regulation becomes increasingly unenforceable – as is the case with banking regulation in the US.

Review of regulations

The conclusion from this is that all regulations should be considered as temporary. Some, such as the prohibition against selling contaminated meat or old fish, we will need as long as we eat animal proteins. In fact, as fish farming will become increasingly a main supplier of animal proteins - and in another fifty years it might well provide as many units of animal protein and as many calories for the world's population as meat does now – we will surely need a substantial number of additional regulations to make sure that only fresh and unspoiled fish is being offered on the world's food markets.

However, any regulation needs to be reviewed fairly often – perhaps every ten or fifteen years – with the questions: would we now still enact it if we did not now have it? And would we still enact it in the same form?

Regulations which penalize enterprises and consumers

Then there is the final and perhaps most important category of regulations that need to be reduced if not eliminated – the regulations which penalize enterprise and penalize the consumer. Such regulation is the wrong way to attain a political objective, even if the objective itself is the right objective at which to aim.

One of the foundations of Japan's rise in the last forty years has been Japan's high savings rate, as everybody knows. But most people seem not to know that Japan historically, before World War II, did not have a high savings rate. On the contrary; a common criticism of Japan's pre-World War II economy was of its inadequately low savings rate, especially as Japan was a rapidly-developing country. It is simply nonsense to say, as a good many American observers now do, that the Japanese 'traditionally' are high savers – traditionally, ever since Tokugawa days, Japanese have been low savers. What made them into high savers around 1950, forty five years ago, was a deliberate attempt to make savings attractive – which the Postal Savings Account did in a particularly successful and, indeed, in a particularly elegant form.

But at the same time, Japanese government policy tried to increase the savings rate by penalizing consumption through regulations that made consumer goods expensive; that is, by limiting competition in retail, and by forbidding discounting. All this did was to saddle Japan with unnecessarily high costs and to perpetuate an increasingly ineffective distribution system.

Encouraging savings was the right thing to do. Penalizing effective distribution was the wrong thing to do. The Japanese consumer have shown clearly over these last few years what their preferences are. In fact, now that Japan is a high wage country, the only way to maintain Japan's competitiveness in the World Economy is by bringing down the cost of living – and this is what an effective distribution system does.

The fewer the better

To sum up: it is not that regulations are necessary or unnecessary – that depends on the individual regulation. To be sure, the fewer regulations the better. An old proverb of the Roman Law, by now over two thousand years old, says: 'Many laws make for very poor Law.' This is still true. Many regulations make for very poor regulation. But what is important, above all, is that we avoid regulations that do harm. These are, first, regulations that are not enforceable. Secondly, they are regulations that have outlived their usefulness, regulations that have outlived the assumptions under which they were enacted. Finally – the largest single category – we need to avoid and to repeal regulations which penalize economic activity, whether production or consumption.

March 10, 1995

The initiative has to come from government and its policy has to be transnational
Peter Drucker

Small government

In all Western countries – and soon, surely in Japan, too – we are working on shrinking government. The British have gone furthest in this direction, but what they have actually done is not so much to shrink government as to move government work from fully-owned governmental agencies into more-or-less autonomous and semi-privatized ones. In the US we are now trying very hard to cut back on a government which has clearly grown out of all proportion and beyond our capacity to support it. In Japan, too, I suspect, we will soon see strong efforts to cut back on government. Government in all developed countries has grown much too fast since World War II, and as a result, has become less effective rather than more effective.

But the goal is not a weak government. It must be a strong and effective government. New political tasks are waiting for us that will require more government effectiveness, greater government vision, and stronger government leadership.

Beyond a single nation

For the first time in history, we now face political challenges which cannot be tackled on the basis of what they mean for this or that country alone. These challenges have to be tack-

171

led on the basis of what they mean for all humanity. These are challenges that arise out of the increased technological power in the hands of mankind. They are also challenges that arise out of the tremendous increase in the human population – to the point where, for the first time in the history of the earth, human beings can no longer go about their own business without concerning themselves with the fate of all the other creatures on our planet, and with the fate of the planet itself. These new tasks transcend every individual nation. Yet they are tasks that have to be done by national governments working together.

Money has become transnational

One such challenge has already been mentioned: money has become transnational and cannot be controlled any longer by any national government. There may be a need for a transnational monetary agency – something analogous to the central bank, as it was invented first in England in the late seventeenth century, with the foundation of the Bank of England in 1694, worked through theoretically and practically in England and France in the first half of the nineteenth century, and then between 1844 and 1914 extended to all countries. Alternatively, we may need a confederation of central banks.

Free banking

We may even find that, as the small but growing group of 'free banking' theorists in major universities asserts, the world monetary scene is so complex and moves so fast that no regulation can possibly work, so that there has to be a completely free market. This would mean abolition of all central banks, and of all regulation of banking and money.

I doubt that any country is ready for such a radical departure. I also very much doubt that it could work – at least not unless we return to metallic currency and get rid of paper money. However, the very fact that 'free banking' is taken seriously by first-rate economists – and in fact even by some experienced commercial bankers – shows that we face an unprecedented situation in respect to one of the central pillars of government: control of money. One thing one can say quite unambiguously: what the monetary bureaucracies in the major countries – the Bank of Japan; the Federal Reserve Board in the US; the Deutsche Bank; the Banque de France;

the Bank of England – are now trying to do is not going to be the permanent answer. They are trying to pretend that they are still in control – and at the first crisis, we see that this no longer works. Then they try to pretend that working together they can be in control – and at the first crisis, this does not work, either. Yet these are the ablest people, and the most experienced people around. That they have so little success in trying to maintain the traditional system shows that we face a fundamental challenge.

Transnational issue of the environment

An equally daunting challenge, though of a totally different nature, is presented by the need to protect the environment. For the first time, actions taken within one territory threaten all of humanity, every place and, in fact, all life on this earth. The destruction of the rain forest in the Amazon, or of the ozone layer in the atmosphere affects everyone. The actions themselves are local, such as the cutting and burning of the trees in the Amazon, or a discharge of carbofluorides by the individual household. The effect is not local, however. Nor – as we thought only a few years ago – can the environment be protected by action on the part of the main developed countries themselves, the countries that have the wealth to pay for environmental protection. The Soviet Union, it now turns out, has been the worst environmental threat – and the threat is concentrated in the poorest parts of Russian Asia. Similarly, Mainland China, as it develops, will pose environmental threats beyond anything anybody now imagines. Here, the question of transnational action that both protects the environment and benefits poor countries desperately in need of rapid economic growth, will become a major task, especially for the governments of the developed countries.

Horrors of civil war

So will the growing threat of international terrorism. Closely related to it is the question of what to do with the horrors of civil war: a Bosnia, a Rwanda, a Somalia, a Cambodia, and so on. Can these massacres still be looked upon as local and as something the rest of the world can - and perhaps must - ignore and disregard? Or do they pose such threats to all humanity, that they require common action? So far, we have not been able to make up our minds. So far, we have not been able to think through what, if anything, could be done.

The record of 'Peace Keeping' by the UN has been very spotty. When Iraq assaulted Kuwait there was near-unanimity that aggression had to be stopped, and the US was able to take effective action. In Bosnia, Rwanda and Somalia there has been neither unanimity nor effective action. Can effective action be taken without unanimity? Can and should it be taken by one major power acting on behalf of the world community – which is the way we tackled Iraq? All these are questions that no one can answer as yet. But surely they will become major challenges, for the simple reason that today every family in its own home sees these horrors on its own television screen. They are no longer far away and something one only reads about in the history books thirty years later. They are personal experiences. They are things that happen to a neighbor. Can one disregard them?

How should they be handled – can they be handled at all?

Failure of the attempt to stop nuclear proliferation

The two attempts at transnational action so far have been very disappointing. In fact, both have been failures. One was the attempt to stop nuclear proliferation. It was the one area in which, even at the peak of the Cold War, the US and the Soviet Union worked together, and fairly closely. Whatever their disagreements, the superpowers were united in their goal of stopping the proliferation of atomic weapons. The attempt has been unsuccessful. In addition to the original nuclear powers – the US, the UK, and the Soviet Union – there are now France, Mainland China, and Israel, and there are also (almost certainly) Argentina, Iran, Iraq, Pakistan, India and North Korea.

Failure of international economic aid

Equally alarming is the lack of success of international economic aid. Development Aid, invented by President Truman in 1950 – is surely one of the most innovative ideas of this century. It has, however, been a total failure. The countries that have actually developed got either no aid at all, or practically none – as is the case with Japan and of all of Southeast Asia. The countries that have received the most aid – chiefly Africa – have had no or little development. This has not only been true of direct government-to-government aid. The enormous amounts of money the World Bank has invested in development have also had a minimal effect. We understand the reasons why – the aid has either been misused to finance military extravagance (as with so much of the governmental aid to Latin America and to Africa), or it has been misused to build economic extravagances (such as enormous steel mills for which there is no market).

Needs of economic aid

Yet there is need for poor countries to develop rapidly. One reason is that we now know that rapid economic development is possible. Another is that the world's inequality is no longer tenable; it is totally different from the economic inequalities of the past.

As far back as we have any historical record, there have always been rich people and poor people in any given country. The inequality between the two was much greater in the past than it is now. Nothing one could find anywhere today, in any developed country, comes remotely close to the inequality between the unbelievable luxury of the Courtiers and Princes in *Genji Monogatari* (I just reread it with great enjoyment) and the peasants and woodcutters of that time, a thousand years ago. But historically there was never much difference between the inequality in one country and the inequality in any other country. Heian Japan was neither more nor less equal than Song China or Charlemagne's Europe. However, today the poorest in a rich country are infinitely richer than all but a very small number of the very, very richest in the truly poor countries. Modern information has made this inequality visible, and thereby intolerable.

At the same time we know that it is not that the poor countries have become poorer. It is not, as nineteenth and early twentieth century Marxism maintained, a question of exploitation. In fact, nothing has been disproved as completely as the so-called 'dependency theory' – the sophisticated version of the old 'Imperialism' slogan which became popular, especially in Latin America, thirty or forty years ago. The rapid rise of very poor countries in Southeast Asia – but also the rapid turn-around of Latin American countries as soon as they switched to a Free Market Economy – has shown that there are no rich countries and poor countries anymore. There are only well-managed countries and badly-managed countries.

The market forces

With respect to economic development it can be agreed that the task can – and should – be done by market forces. Local government, whether of Singapore or of Chile, has to create the right social and economic conditions, and then the market will do the rest.

Market forces can play a role in preserving the environment. It is surely more intelligent to make protecting the environment economically attractive for consumers, farmers and small businesses than it is to impose penalties.

Initiative of government

However, the initiative has to come from governments – and policy will have to be transnational. Control of nuclear proliferation or suppression of transnational terrorism cannot be left to market forces either.

A central question is thus surely the effectiveness of government. What can government actually do well?

This, it can confidently be predicted, will be a central concern of the next decades – and our survival is at issue.

March 10, 1995

Old political theory has collapsed. Government has to re-think to transform itself into 'effective government'
Peter Drucker

GLOBAL ISSUES ARE ONLY ONE PART of the challenges to government. Government faces equal challenges in its traditional domestic role. In fact, we are at the point where we will have to reinvent government.

Three-hundred-year old political theories

Our basic political theories are now some three hundred years old. They go back to the England of the late seventeenth century, and to such people as John Locke. All the theories we have concern themselves with the question, 'What should government do? And how should it do it?' No-one, for over three hundred years, has asked, "What can government do?" (The last one to ask this in the West was Machiavelli in the early sixteenth century). Yet, this is clearly the question we have to tackle, and soon.

Japan and Europe

Japan, it should be said, still has the most effective government of all developed countries, but this is not, as so many 'Japan Bashers' in the US believe, because Japanese government is unique. On the contrary, it is largely because Japan, of all developed countries, has the most traditional government. The Japanese relationship between government and the economy is, for instance, not very different from the French relationship or from the German relationship. In fact, what the French call *dirigisme* is exactly what the Japanese call 'administrative guidance' – except that the French *dirigisme* is far more controlling than Japanese 'administrative guidance' has been. And French agricultural protectionism is far more protective than Japanese agricultural protectionism is or ever was. Altogether the features in Japanese government and politics which are considered 'uniquely Japanese' by most analysts in the US are features which, prior to World War I, characterized all governments on the European continent – and still characterize most of them.

The power of bureaucracy

The 'Japan Bashers' in the US point out, for instance, that

177

the bureaucracy runs the country, and not the politicians. But this was just as true of continental Europe until quite recently – in fact, it still is largely true. The Japan Bashers point out that in Japan the ablest of the young people go into government service, and that government service enjoys tremendous social standing and respect. But this is still largely true in Continental Europe – in Germany, for instance. In France, the lower rungs of the bureaucracy are treated with ridicule and contempt, but the upper civil servants are considered to be supermen – deities rather than ordinary human beings. The Japan Bashers point out as a peculiarity of Japan, that Japanese senior civil servants do not retire, but 'descend from Heaven' into top jobs in business. I happen to come from a civil-service family in Austria-Hungary which until 1918, (that is until well after my birth), was a great power. Every one of the three senior civil servants who, as 'Vice Ministers', ran the Austria-Hungarian war economy during World War I (one of them was my father), 'retired' at age forty five or fifty to become the chairman of a major bank. A senior civil servant in Germany retires today around age fifty, to become a highly paid director-general of an industry association – and (as in Japan), industry associations in Germany are where the power is. The senior civil servant in France, the *Inspecteur de Finance*, 'retires' at around age forty five to take over the top management of a major company – and so on.

Japanese government is the most traditional

Above all, Japan is the most traditional of all governments around, in that it is the only government of any developed country that has, by and large, stayed out of trying to run the social sphere. It has – successfully – tried to control the economy without running it. It has tried to manage society, but without running it. This is what all European governments did before 1933 and especially before 1914.

This explains why Japanese government is still far more effective than any other. Even so, the effectiveness of government – even in Japan – is rapidly diminishing. And for the same reason: we do not know what government can do. Therefore governments try to do far too many things which they cannot do, or cannot do well.

Two things required to renew government

To answer the question on what government can do will, in

the end, require new political theory. However, right away it will require the same two things that are required to renew a business enterprise: (1) building continuing improvement into government; and (2) concentrating government on what works, and abandoning what does not work.

Continuous improvement is considered a recent Japanese invention – the Japanese call it *kaizen*. But in fact it was invented almost eighty years ago, and in the US. From World War I until the early 1980s when it was dissolved, the American Telephone Company (the Bell System) applied 'continuous improvement' to every one of its activities and processes, whether it was installing a telephone in a home or manufacturing switchgear. For every one of these activities Bell defined results, performance, quality, and cost. For everyone it set an annual improvement goal. Bell managers were not rewarded for reaching these goals. Those who did not reach them were out of the running, and were rarely given a second chance.

Benchmarking

What is equally needed – and is also an old Bell Telephone invention – is 'benchmarking': every year comparing the performance of an operation or an agency with the performances of all others, with the best becoming the standard to be met by all the following year.

Continuous improvement and benchmarking are largely unknown in government agencies. They would require radical changes in policies and practices which the bureaucracy would fiercely resist. They would require every agency – and every bureau within it – to define its performance objective, its quality objective, and its cost objective. It would require defining the results that the agency is supposed to produce.

The system of compensation

Moreover, continuous improvement and benchmarking need different incentives. An agency that did not improve its performance by a preset minimum would have its budget cut – which was Bell Telephone's approach. A bureau chief whose unit consistently falls below the benchmark set by the best performers would be penalized in terms of compensation or – more effectively – in terms of eligibility for promotion. Non-performers would ultimately be demoted or fired.

Need to re-think organization

But not even such changes, though they would be considered radical by almost anybody in any bureaucracy, would warrant being called a reinvention of government. Things that should not be done at all are always done worst – and thus we always see the greatest improvements in doing better what should not be done at all.

Any organization, whether biological or social, needs to change its basic structure if it changes its size significantly. Any organization that doubles or triples in size needs to be re-thought. Similarly, any organization, be it a business, a nonprofit organization, or a government agency, needs to re-think itself once it is more than forty or fifty years old. It has outgrown its policies and its rules of behavior. If it continues in its old ways, it becomes ungovernable, unmanageable, uncontrollable.

In the US today, but equally in Europe, we talk a good deal about 'downsizing' government. To be sure, government in all Western countries has become so big as to be unwieldy. But before we can downsize we need to re-think.

'Would we now go into this mission?'

In the US a few organizations – for instance, a few large companies and a few large hospitals – have actually demonstrated ways of doing this. These organizations knew that to start by reducing expenditure is not the way to control costs. The starting point is to identify the activities that are productive, that should be strengthened, promoted, and expanded. Every agency, every policy, every program, every activity, should be confronted with these questions: 'What is your mission?' 'Is it still the right mission?' 'Is it still worth doing?' 'If we were not already doing this, would we now go into it?' This procedure has been done often enough in all kinds of American organizations – businesses, hospitals, churches, and even local governments – to convince us that it works.

The overall answer is almost never 'This agency or this program is fine as it stands; let's keep on.' but in some – indeed, a good many – areas the answer to the question is 'Yes, we would go into this again, but with some changes. We have learned a few things.'

But in many cases the conclusion will be that a given agency or policy is no longer viable, if it ever was. We would definitely not start it now if we had the choice.

Or there may be no mission left. For example, would any developed country now establish a separate Ministry of Agriculture when farmers are no more than 3 per cent or 4 per cent of the population? A good many Americans would answer with a loud 'No.'

Some perfectly respectable activities belong elsewhere. A good many government agencies in developed countries surely deserve to be privatized.

Wasteful activities

Continuing activities that we would not now start is wasteful. They should be abandoned. One cannot even guess how many government activities would be found worth preserving. But my experience with many organizations suggests that the public would vote against continuing something like two-fifths, if not half, of all civilian agencies and programs of the present American government. Almost none of them would win an unqualified 'Yes' vote by a large margin, that is, would be deemed to be properly organized and operating well.

The thorny cases are the programs and activities that are unproductive or counterproductive without our quite knowing what is wrong, let alone how to fix it.

Two major and highly cherished US government programs belong in this category.

The US welfare program

The US welfare program is one highly visible example. When it was designed in the late 1930s it worked beautifully. But the needs it then tackled were different from those it is supposed to serve today – the needs of unwed mothers and fatherless children, of people without education, skills, or work experience. Whether it actually does harm is hotly debated. But few would claim that it works or that it alleviates the social ills it is supposed to cure.

Military aid

Then there is that mainstay of US foreign policy during the Cold War years: military aid. If it is given to an ally who is actually engaged in fighting, military aid can be highly productive; consider Lend-Lease to Great Britain in 1940-41, and military aid to an embattled Israel. But military aid is counterproductive if it is given in peacetime to an ally – something Plutarch and Suetonius already accepted as proven in Roman Antiquity. Surely the worst recent foreign policy messes of the US – Panama, Iran, Iraq, and Somalia are prime examples – were caused by our giving military aid to create an ally. Little, if any, military aid since the beginning of the Cold War has actually produced an ally. Indeed, it usually produced an enemy – as did Soviet military aid to Afghanistan.

To reform or to abolish

The favorite prescription for such programs or activities is to reform them, but to reform something that malfunctions (let alone something that does harm) without knowing why it does not work can only make things worse. The best thing to do with such programs is to abolish them.

Re-thinking will result in a list, with activities and programs that should be strengthened at the top; activities that should be abolished at the bottom; and in between, activities that need to be refocused or in which a few hypotheses might be tested. Some activities and programs should, despite an absence of results, be given a grace period of a few years before they are put out of their misery. In the US, welfare may be the prime example.

Great by-product – cost savings

Re-thinking is not primarily concerned with cutting expenses. It leads above all to a tremendous increase in performance, in quality and in service. But substantial cost savings – sometimes as much as 40 per cent of the total – always emerge as a by-product. In fact, re-thinking could produce enough savings to eliminate the Federal deficit in the US within a few years. The main result, however, would be a change in the basic approach. Where conventional policy-making ranks programs and activities according to their good intentions, re-thinking ranks them according to results.

It seems to be impossible today

Anyone who has read this far will exclaim, 'Impossible. Surely no group of people will ever agree on what belongs at the top of the list and what at the bottom.' But, amazingly enough, wherever re-thinking has been done, there has been substantial agreement about the list, whatever the backgrounds or the beliefs of the people involved. The disagreements are rarely over what should be strengthened and what should be abandoned. They are usually over whether a program or activity should be killed right away or put on probation for two or three years.

But, as will be argued, even total agreement among highly respectable people will be futile. The politicians will not accept anything like this. Neither will the bureaucracy. And lobbyists and special interests of all persuasions will be united in opposition to anything so 'subversive.'

It is perfectly true: radical re-thinking of government seems impossible today. Even patching is exceedingly difficult, as witness the snail's speed at which political reform moves in Japan.

Will it be impossible tomorrow?

Will such re-thinking be impossible tomorrow? In every developed country there is a crisis of government today. The public is totally disenchanted. And in a crisis, one needs a plan. In a crisis, one turns to people who have thought through in advance what needs to be done. Of course, no plan, no matter how well thought through, will ever be carried out as written. But such a plan could serve as the ideal against which the compromises are measured. It might save us from sacrificing things that should be strengthened in order to maintain the obsolete and the unproductive. It would not guarantee that all – or even most – of the unproductive things would be cut. But it might maintain the productive ones.

Effective government

In fact, we may already be very close to having to reinvent government. For it has become clear that a developed country can neither extend big government, as the (so-called) liberals want, nor abolish it and go back to nineteenth century innocence, as the (so-called) conservatives want. The government we need will have to transcend both groups. The megastate that this century built is bankrupt, morally as well as financially. It has not delivered. But its successor cannot be 'small government.' There are far too many tasks, domestically and internationally. We need effective government – and that is what the voters in all developed countries are actually clamoring for.

Of course Japanese government is different from any other

in many ways – but so is every government. What all of them have in common is that the theory on which they are based, the political theory of the last three hundred years, has run its course. In every country, therefore, governments are becoming less effective when we need them to become more effective. In every country the question of what government can do is rapidly becoming the central question – and one which nobody has yet taken seriously or has yet studied.

For this reason, the conclusion of this dialogue has to be that reinventing government will become the most important of all the issues Mr Nakauchi and I have been discussing.

March 10, 1995

Government must adopt an approach to economic policy that is oriented to the private sector
Isao Nakauchl

Challenges to create a brighter future

Your replies have given me and other Japanese executives hope and courage. May I take this opportunity to confess the deepest respect for your perceptive insight?

Although I have said this countless times it bears repeating; your wisdom has taught us how to be courageous in challenging the many tasks we must deal with now and in the future, and increasing a brighter future. You have also shown us that it is our duty to achieve this. I believe that those of us directly engaged in business management have a particularly heavy responsibility with respect to the free market economy, deregulation, and the role of government.

First, I should like briefly to set out my views with respect to your own on recreating the free market economy and the role of government.

Based on market economies

As you are of course well aware, industrial policy in Japan, while highly successful in rebuilding and advancing the economy after the war, has created many problems. A typical example is the price differentials between domestic and overseas markets, particularly in foodstuffs. Government regulations that restrict market access and prevent prices from falling must be eliminated immediately, and executives throughout the nation must strive to modernize the distribution structure as quickly as possible. Otherwise, the Japanese people will never be able to enjoy true material well-being.

Countries that embrace democracy, liberalization, and market economic principles are steadily gathering under a WTO (World Trade Organization) umbrella of comprehensive rules governing international trade and investment. In this context it is not only unacceptable but unfeasible for an industrialized country such as Japan to maintain economic regulations which violate market principles, simply in order to protect domestic industries that lack international competitiveness. As you pointed out, Japan's role is to contribute actively to the development of a new global economic order based on market economies that maximize opportunity and minimize failure.

I also agree that the development of emerging economies must be achieved through private sector activity rather than Official Development Assistance (ODA).

Japanese administration

I have been stressing time after time the need for a drastic 'zero base' (only where absolutely necessary) approach to scrapping regulations in order to reform Japanese systems. Fortunately this view is shared by Japanese industry. The unfortunate reality is that the government does little more than support the status quo; there has been very little progress in reviewing regulations governing economic activities, as you have recommended, let alone in the reform of systems.

I believe that this can be attributed to the fact that the Japanese government is not prepared to discuss the very basic question of what government can do. Your observation is the same as mine: governments try to do far too many things that they either cannot do or cannot do well. The Japanese administration is still clearly attempting to preserve outdated and outmoded systems. I believe that it is vitally important for the government to stop thinking this way.

185

Awareness of being citizens

The Great Hanshin-Awaji Earthquake has shown many Japanese that the government cannot protect the lives and property of the people. The government is still unable to fulfill even the basic everyday needs of residents in stricken areas. The administrative response in the aftermath of the quake has been so slow that even now, two months after the disaster, only the bare minimum of temporary housing has been forthcoming, and many people still have no option but to stay in evacuation centers. More people are realizing that they cannot rely on a government that does nothing for them.

On a visit to the quake area, I found myself disillusioned; the administration was unable to provide an appropriate response to the needs of the people. It made me pessimistic and at one stage nihilistic about the future. It was then that I remembered your words of nearly sixty years ago, near the end of *The End of Economic Man:* 'The masses turn to fascism because they are in despair.' I completely agree. More than anything else, we must never lose hope if we are to shield ourselves from the threat of fascism and our people from misfortune.

To achieve this, both individuals and enterprises must strive as citizens to meet the challenge head-on with every ounce of wisdom and courage. They must embrace the principle of individual and corporate responsibility, eliminate outdated systems wedded to Japanese economics and society that hinder the process of change, and develop a new economy and society and a brighter future for all. As we have seen in Kobe, people must endeavor to channel their feelings about an ineffectual administration into a positive perception of themselves as autonomous citizens, rather than both parties attempting to blame one another for the rising level of mutual distrust.

Systems that should be reformed

I believe that reforming outdated systems represents our first and most important task if we are to change Japan by boosting an awareness of citizenship. You nominated the Ministry of Agriculture as an example of an obsolete department; in Japan there are also vestiges of old systems that should have been challenged long ago but which remains stubbornly at the core of our society.

By this I am referring to the wartime administrative structure of the 1940s, designed to give the central government control over people, materials and money to prosecute the war. Specific examples include the National General Mobilization Law, which led in turn to the Food Control Law (designed to ensure total government control over production and distribution of food), the Bank of Japan Law (designed to achieve the national objectives of the central bank) and the withholding tax system that prevents the Japanese people from realizing themselves as taxpayers. I am convinced that these systems rob the Japanese people of the spirit of autonomy. You said that the Japanese government did not intrude particularly heavily into the social arena, but it appears that, most regrettably, Japanese government does so systematically.

Developing a citizen's society

If we accept the above, then stimulating economic activity through deregulation, while very important in itself, represents no more than a secondary issue. The true goal of deregulation-based administrative reform should be to purge the wartime structure and mentality and create societies based on private initiatives through structural reform, rather than simply to effect legislative changes. This is necessary if we are to create a true citizen's society. In this sense, I believe that getting rid of the wartime administrative structure should be the aim of every member of the Japanese public, not just industry and government. This is at once incredibly simple but requiring of extraordinary effort; it also represents the only means of successfully developing our society into a true citizen's society. The government should address this task immediately, and resolve to see it through.

Influence of new Keynesian scholars

I should like here to lay down my thoughts based on the lessons you taught me. What should the government, industry and people of Japan do, particularly what should Japanese executives do, to build a citizen's society? First, the government must adopt a private-sector-oriented approach to economic and particularly fiscal policy.

In your book *The Ecological Vision* you maintain that Japanese economic policies are not based on Keynesian principles. However, the Japanese government is clearly influenced by these principles or, more accurately, by the teachings of new Keynesian scholars. This is similar to what you described in your work, *'Keynes: Economics as a Magical System,'* 'his very disciples, while using Keynesian terms, methods and tools, were abandoning his economic policies and arms.' This influence is evident in government economic policies formulated from the economic model developed by the Economic Planning Agency.

As I understand it, Keynesian and neo-Keynesian economic theory sees government as a collection of learned individuals who, in order to create economic stability, must lead the ignorant masses, whose disorderly behavior in turn restricts the scope of policy. In reality, of course, those in government cannot openly claim to be the elite, nor can they brand the masses ignorant. Whether consciously or unconsciously, the government sees its mission as protecting the masses from threats and leading them forward. This is a highly dangerous line for government to take, as it prevents people from becoming aware of their personal responsibilities and amplifies the impact of its errors.

Shift to free market economy based on personal responsibility

As it happens, the ability of the Japanese government to influence the economy is rapidly diminishing. This is particularly evident in the field of fiscal policy.

The Japanese government has implemented over 45 trillion yen in economic measures over the last two years. One could even expect economic inflation as the result. However, it did not cause the economic recovery in Japan. Nevertheless the popular myth of public works investment remains as sacred as always, and the allocation of even 0.1 per cent of the total attracts heated debate in political, economic, bureaucratic and journalistic circles. Such discussion might be useful if it examined purposeful social infrastructure improvement, but to examine only the potential impact on economic activity is of little or no benefit, I think.

Although there are many reasons why these economic measures have failed to produce the intended results, I believe that it suggests that the days of government-led fiscal policy are over. It shows that we need to make the transition toward genuine private-sector-led policies.

Thus, now is the time for the Japanese economy to move away from the central government-controlled economic model dependent on public works investment, and maximize the benefits of a market economy under a dynamic free competition model founded on the principle of the personal responsibility of participants. This is also necessary to avoid repeating the mistakes of a planned economy, which failed by attempting to exert complete centralized controls.

Information for innovation

Next, private enterprise must continually develop new customers through sustained innovation.

Innovation is not something that requires a special set of circumstance to suddenly spring up one day out of nothing. As I wrote earlier, my own experience suggests that innovation arises from an ability to combine accurately information on global developments and consumer needs with a knowledge of human resources, and all other business management resources available to the enterprise. There is nothing special about this; it comes from sustained, everyday effort. I also believe that information on innovation is derived from the very field where one operates; in the retailing industry, this means within and outside the stores that customers visit. In the same way, information about non-customers who do not visit is even more important in creating new customers, as you point out.

The meaning of innovation is thus clear: it is an ideal rather than just a strategy. It involves sifting through outside information, understanding customers, and accurately evaluating and responding to market needs regularly under a single, clearly-enunciated ideal. At Daiei, for instance, the ideal is 'For the Customers,' by satisfying their needs through understanding their needs through direct and indirect communications with existing and potential customers.

Anecdotes of two leaders – Sadaharu Oh

The mission of executives as leaders is to instill in themselves and in their organizations an attitude and a climate conducive to innovation, as spelled out in detail in your published works and through our written exchanges.

Finally, I whould like to present here anecdotes regarding two organizational leaders who are my close acquaintances, to illustrate my feelings about the prerequisites for executives and the importance of leadership.

The first is Sadaharu Oh, field manager of my professional

baseball team the Fukuoka Daiei Hawks. He is one of the most famous batters in baseball history in both Japan and the world, as he holds the world record for the aggregate of home runs.

Oh has always said that he 'never had time to enjoy the afterglow of hitting a home run. I was always wondering about whether I would be able to hit the ball next time at the batter box and what sort of hit I would make. I would be sorting through the information in my mind to find what I needed to know about how the pitcher and the ball would behave.' The words are highly significant in illustrating the qualities of people we can call true professionals.

Oh kept a vast store of information for his own use. He would store, analyze and collate in his own way the information about the many and various pitchers he had faced in the past. This practice, which made him the world leader in home runs, was partly a response to his unusual predicament as a top batter: he had fewer opportunities to hit because pitchers, fearful of his skill, deliberately sent him to walk. During his career as a player, Oh scored a record 2,390 bases on balls, some 1,116 more than the second record-holder. These incredible statistics, which place him firmly in the league of legendary batters, translate into an average of 0.88 bases on balls per game (also a record, the number 2 figure being just 0.51). Oh was forced to maximize his limited opportunities by analyzing and storing information to improve his batting figures and contribute to the team.

The tale of Sadaharu Oh tells us something about the duties of executives and leaders. My own interpretation is that the legendary Oh has written his name in the Japanese professional baseball history books and won the admiration of young baseball fans then and now, by faithfully and unwaveringly carrying through the following five principles from his batting days through to the present.

The five are: (1) sorting through a vast range of information that constitutes experience, and storing this in meaningful and readily usable form; (2) utilizing this information to make the most of limited opportunities by posing hypotheses about each pitcher before reaching the plate; (3) reevaluating the results of each turn at the bat and storing this new information in readiness for the next turn; (4) employing and continuing a cycle of hypothesis, execution and validation, and

(5) endeavoring to utilize his wealth of experience to teach young baseball players and nurture the great batters and pitchers of tomorrow.

Sadaharu Oh has demonstrated that a person who possesses a wealth of information can implement the hypothesis-execution-validation cycle described above, and pass on the associated lessons to those following. They can then utilize their own personal experiences in nurturing the executives of tomorrow. The person who can do this is a true executive and professional.

Anecdotes of a second leader – Arie Selinger

The other organizational leader I want to mention is Arie Selinger, the first head coach ever to take the Daiei volleyball team through to league victory in March this year. As a national team head coach, Selinger won silver medals for the American Girls' Team in the 1984 Los Angeles Olympics and the Netherlands Men's Team in the Barcelona Olympics in 1992. He became head coach of the Daiei Orange Attackers in 1989.

It happened in the match where our team clinched the league-victory. The Daiei team had already lost two consecutive sets to their opponents and was in a seemingly hopeless situation. As you may know, in volleyball the first team to take three sets is the winner. Everyone thought that Daiei was finished, even the players. It was at this point that Selinger gathered the dispirited team around him and said, 'We've still got three sets to go.'

His positive words changed the mood of the team instantly, wiping out the 'one more set and we're gone' feeling and replacing it with the spirit of 'let's start afresh and win three sets.' The team went on to take the three sets and garner an impressive victory. This short episode illustrates the tremendous importance of what leaders should say.

If the leader had said, 'There's only one set to go; if we lose this it's all over', with his team driven into such a difficult position, what would have happened? The players would have felt completely cornered and even more dejected and the game would have been lost before long. But 'We've still got three sets to go' successfully planted the spirit of challenge in each player's heart, got rid of the atmosphere of defeat, and united the team in the quest for victory.

The players were uplifted by positive rather than harsh words. This is equally true in companies, as I know from many years' experience. Since the recent earthquake, I encouraged staff overwhelmed by the sheer scale of the disaster not to cry over spilt milk but instead to think positively and work quickly at the task of restoration for the sake of loyal Daiei customers.

The spirit of any organization is affected for better or worse by the words of its leader. Executives must be made aware of this fact. I believe that Arie Selinger's example shows how we can impart courage and determination.

Developing one's strength

It is not easy to become an executive like Sadaharu Oh and Arie Selinger, but neither is it impossible if we strive to develop our own strengths. This is where your teachings, which draw on your wealth of experience and critical appraisal of humanity, are so valuable. Your teachings may seem extremely simple at first glance, but they require an uncommon level of effort to achieve. But I must repeat: it is possible.

It is my sincere hope that as many of us as possible may become 'effective executives,' that is, executives who will make extraordinary efforts to reinvent themselves, facing difficult challenges with wisdom and courage, and will make the world different by addressing the tasks before them. I believe that you and I agree on this point.

The duty of executives

Through our exchange of letters, Professor Drucker, you have given me and other Japanese executives profound advice, and through this identified the tasks that we must address to create the future. You have set us a difficult but appealing challenge. It is the duty of executives and the 'executives of tomorrow' to meet this challenge. After all, the problem is our own; we must create the future by ourselves.

As an executive charged with this tremendous responsibility for the future, I pledge to you and our readers that I will work with many other executives to follow the instructions that I have received from you. I will strive to fulfill your expectations by continuing to contribute to the process of creating the future as I have up till now.

March 27, 1995

ifth Generation Management
)ynamic Teaming, Virtual Enterprising and Knowledge Networking
Second Edition

Charles Savage Digital Equipment Corporation

his revised edition of *Fifth Generation Management* helps executives out of the rigid mindsets of the Industrial Era into the vibrant and invigorating possibilities of co-creation in the Knowledge Era.

- Over 25,000 copies of previous edition sold
  Previous edition was awarded 'Book of the Year' by Tom Peters
- Covers lessons learned over the last five years since *Fifth Generation Management* was first published
- Includes discussion of 'antibodies' resisting meaningful change in organizations
  Emphasizes dynamic teaming of core capabilities – in the context of 'Intellectual capital' and 'Knowledge Assets'
  Includes coverage of virtual enterprising in the Knowledge Era

CONTENTS: Preface by Tom Peters; Preface to Revised Edition; Preface (Original); PART 1: Customer Empowerment: Reinventing our Enterprises in Six Months; January: bosses or customers?; February: routines or capabilities; March: individuals or teams?; April: being seen or seeing: May: power or energy?; June: reflection in reinvention?; PART 2: Dynamic Teaming, Virtual Enterprising and Knowledge Networking; Introduction: our past and future; Five generations of computers and management; Computerizing enterprises; Steep hierarchies: our burden; Elegantly simple enterprises; Leading knowledge networking; Lean, agile, robust and spirited enterprising; Afterword: Daniel Burris; Chapter Notes; References; Index.

7506 9701 6   April 1996   256pp   Paperback

Creating Organizational Advantage
WINNER OF THE MCA BOOK PRIZE

Colin Egan
Professor of Strategic Management, Leicester Business School

Creating Organizational Advantage presents a critical appraisal of fashions and fads in managment theory. It exposes the strategic weaknesses of change programmes such as Total Quality Management and Business Process Re-Engineering and explains why so many companies fail to become 'market-led' or customer-focused'.

'This is an insightful work which covers a great deal of territory in an accessible style. It does not provide quick-fix solutions but it raises several key issues and provides food for thought. This helps explain why it won the Management Consultancies Association's prize for the best management book for 1995.' Financial Times

0 7506 1937 6   1995   224pp   Illustrated   Paperback

BUTTERWORTH HEINEMANN

A division of Reed Educational and Professional Publishing Ltd, Linacre House, Jordan Hill, Oxford OX2 8DP
Tel: +44 (0)1865 310366   Fax: +44 (0)1865 310898

EASY ORDERING
Please Quote ref.
T601BGBA01

UK	US	Singapore
Heinemann Customer Services	Butterworth-Heinemann	Reed Academic Publishing Asia
Direct Mail Department	225 Wildwood Avenue	1 Temasek Avenue
PO Box 840	Woburn	#17-01
Oxford	MA 01801	Millenia Tower
OX2 8YW	Tel: 1-800-366-2665	Singapore 039192
Tel: 01865 314627		Tel: 65 338 3006

Supergrowth Companies
Entrepreneurs in Action
John Harrison
Management Consultant
Bernard Taylor
Professor of Business Policy and Executive Director of the Centre for Board Effectiveness, Henley Management College
with Ann Todd and Mahen Tampoe

Medium-sized high-growth companies provide much of the momentum for national economic growth. They are the vanguard of change in any economy. This is a lively accessible study focusing on medium-sized companies (£20–200 million turnover) which have survived and grown in a rapidly changing marketplace.

- Based on original research from Henley Management College
- Bernard Taylor is the well-known and widely respected author and editor of Long Range Planning
- Medium-sized companies are very much in vogue – as acquisition targets and as having the most growth potential in the future.

CONTENTS: Part 1 – Survival and success in boom and recession; Part 2 – How do you create success?; Part 3 – Can smaller companies thrive internationally?; Part 4 – Summarizing the results; Bibliography; Index.

0 7506 2750 6   September 1996   200pp   Paperback

Managing Mergers, Acquisitions and Strategic Alliances
Integrating People and Cultures
Second Edition
Sue Cartwright
Senior Research Fellow in Organizational Psychology, Manchester School of Management, UMIST
Cary L Cooper
Professor of Organizational Psychology, Manchester School of Management, UMIST

Mergers, acquisitions, and alliances continue to be a feature of the contemporary business scene. The authors assess the contribution that psychology can make to our understanding of the merger phenomena, both in terms of its impact on organizational performance and on the managers and employees involved.

'This is a complex subject which this clearly written, well constructed guide tackles cogently and thoroughly.' – Personnel Today

0 7506 2341 1   1995   256pp   Paperback

BUTTERWORTH HEINEMANN

A division of Reed Educational and Professional Publishing Ltd, Linacre House, Jordan Hill, Oxford OX2 8DP
Tel: +44 (0)1865 310366   Fax: +44 (0)1865 310898

EASY ORDERING
Please Quote ref.
T601BGBA01

UK	US	Singapore
Heinemann Customer Services	Butterworth-Heinemann	Reed Academic Publishing As
Direct Mail Department	225 Wildwood Avenue	1 Temasek Avenue
PO Box 840	Woburn	#17-01
Oxford	MA 01801	Millenia Tower
OX2 8YW	Tel: 1-800-366-2665	Singapore 039192
Tel: 01865 314627		Tel: 65 338 3006